Sermons of Serenity

Pastor Hasan Smith

(Pastor H)

ISBN 979-8-89243-962-6 (paperback)
ISBN 979-8-89243-963-3 (digital)

Christian Faith Publishing
832 Park Avenue
Meadville, PA 16335
www.christianfaithpublishing.com

Printed in the United States of America

In loving memory of my father,
Reverend James R Smith

Satan is the author of confusion.
I, Pastor H, author my offering to you, *Sermons of Serenity.*

**All Scripture is God-breathed and is useful for teaching,
rebuking, correcting and training in righteousness,
so that the servant of God may be thoroughly
equipped for every good work.**

—2 Timothy 3:16–17

Contents

Foreword

Serenity, what is the actual meaning of this word? Serenity means a state of being calm, peaceful, and untroubled. However, we all can probably testify that during these troubled days filled with so much pain, destruction, and evil, this state of mind is difficult to achieve. We seek all sorts of ways to try to gain serenity during these times. I'd like to share with you a blessing that I encountered. I am a person of a particular age, also known as old (LOL). I've experienced a lot, but I have always known the power of GOD in my life. I've been active in organized religion. I've been in and out of church. There have been times where I have questioned my faith. I've read my Bible as well as many other devotionals and inspirational books. Recently, I had the opportunity of being introduced to a book titled, *Sermons of Serenity*. Let me tell you, this book has truly blessed my soul!

Sermons of Serenity deals with real-life issues, concerns, fears, doubts, and situations of today that we all, both believers and non-believers alike, are facing. *Sermons of Serenity* was not written as a replacement for reading the Bible, but more as an inspiration and teaching instrument that encourages you to seek to learn more of God's love, mercy, and grace for us all. Although it deals with the reality of how many view the church, worship, and the religious-based philosophy as a whole, this book is totally backed by Scripture and the Word of God. *Sermons of Serenity* encourages you to want to study the Word and establish a personal relationship with God on your own accord. This book truly blesses as it encourages you to seek the knowledge of God, which will lead you to his peace, the peace that surpasses all understanding as stated in the Word.

A word of introduction to the author. I have personally known this young man all his life. Actually, I gave him life! I've watched him grow from child to man. I've witnessed his trials, tribulations, personal pains, and sufferings. I know that he comes from a place of truth, but most of all a place of love for mankind. His desire in writing this book is to bless us all with another tool that leads us to learn about the love of Jesus Christ and his love for us all! His desire is to assist you in your walk and journey into peace and serenity, which is only achieved through the love of Jesus. Believe me when I say, you don't want to miss the blessings of this book. It is definitely a must-read! Enjoy, *Sermons of Serenity*.

May God bless you.

Patricia Johnson

Preface

When I began New Body of Christ (NBC), the first thing that I wanted to make clear was that this was not just another church! My motivation and desire for differentiating NBC from other churches was driven by a personal realization that "I don't like church!" Now as shocking and bold of a statement as that may seem, especially for a pastor, I assure you that there are countless others, possibly even you, who share this sentiment. I can almost bet that if you were to take an inventory of the people that you know and consider as "good people," encompassing such qualities as being loving, compassionate, supportive and giving, you would find that many of these individuals do not regularly attend or even belong to a church. My father is an example. The sad reality behind this is that many of these people don't want to be associated with us "church folks." I am personally starting to feel as if many churches are turning more people away from God than drawing them to God. Too many Christians have become victims of "church hurt." From the Catholic Church down to the rapid growing nondenominational churches, every sort of offense you can imagine has been committed including such acts as people being misused and conned out of their money, overcontrolling churches that forbid you from visiting other churches as well as talking to family members and friends who have left the church, and the most disgraceful and demonic crimes of pedophilia and sexual abuse scandals, which have destroyed families and left victims with permanent scars. I, like many others, have been a victim of church hurt. I, like many others, have gone to what should be a house of healing and love and instead found terminal spiritual illnesses and hatred. It was in church where

I've witnessed some of the nastiest arguments and fights. It was in church where I've witnessed the evil looks of judgment and condemnation. Now I don't want you to misunderstand what I'm saying. I love God. I've just come to a point in my spiritual walk where I don't like church or at least what the church has become! I want to point out that this issue is nothing new. In the Gospel of Matthew 16, you will find the establishing of the church.

> **When Jesus came into the coasts of Caesarea Philippi, he asked his disciples, saying, Whom do men say that I the Son of man am? And they said, Some say that thou art John the Baptist: some, Elias; and others, Jeremias, or one of the prophets. He saith unto them, But whom say ye that I am? And Simon Peter answered and said, Thou art the Christ, the Son of the living God. And Jesus answered and said unto him, Blessed art thou, Simon Barjona: for flesh and blood hath not revealed it unto thee, but my Father which is in heaven. And I say also unto thee, That thou art Peter, and upon this rock I will build my church; and the gates of hell shall not prevail against it. And I will give unto thee the keys of the kingdom of heaven: and whatsoever thou shalt bind on earth shall be bound in heaven: and whatsoever thou shalt loose on earth shall be loosed in heaven. (Matthew 16:13–19 KJV)**

This was the establishment and is the true church. Now look at what happened no sooner after the church was established. Matthew 16:20–23 reads:

> **Then charged he his disciples that they should tell no man that he was Jesus the**

Christ. From that time forth began Jesus to shew unto his disciples, how that he must go unto Jerusalem, and suffer many things of the elders and chief priests and scribes, and be killed, and be raised again the third day. Then Peter took him, and began to rebuke him, saying, Be it far from thee, Lord: this shall not be unto thee. But he turned, and said unto Peter, Get thee behind me, Satan: thou art an offence unto me: for thou savourest not the things that be of God, but those that be of men. (Matthew 16:20–23 KJV)

I'm afraid that the church is still an offence to Christ, still savoring not the things that are of God, but those that are of men.

The Word of God, however, is ever necessary to our lives, and now even more than ever! In the Bible, Jesus states that, "It is written, Man shall not live by bread alone, but by every word that proceedeth out of the mouth of God" (Matthew 4:4). Second Timothy 3:16–17 (NIV) states that, "All scripture is God-breathed and is useful for teaching, rebuking, correcting and training in righteousness, so that the servant of God may be thoroughly equipped for every good work." I believe that more and more people are beginning to understand this truth, and as a result, people are searching for God like never before. People are looking for help, for knowledge, and for wisdom in the every-day struggles that we all are facing. People want a relationship with God without all the chaos and confusion that sadly enough has become church culture. With all the tragedies upon us, with everything that's going on in the world, with our nation divided, with hearts waxing cold, with so many people giving up, hope is essential! Faith and salvation through Jesus Christ is the only way. The Word of God promises us, "For whosoever shall call upon the name of the Lord shall be saved" (Romans 10:13 KJV). It is in the book of Romans that we learn that faith comes by hearing and hearing by the Word of God (Romans10:17 KJV). The Apostle

Paul also introduces a dilemma explaining, "How then shall they call on him in whom they have not believed? And how shall they believe in him of whom they have not heard? And how shall they hear without a preacher? And how shall they preach, except they be sent? As it is written, How beautiful are the feet of them that preach the gospel of peace, and bring glad tidings of good things" (Roman 10:14–15 KJV)! It is with this biblical truth that God called me to both start New Body of Christ and later to write this first edition of *Sermons of Serenity*.

In preparation for our first service at NBC, one method of advertisement that we used were church flyers. My target audience for attendees at NBC were the people that I just spoke of who didn't regularly attend or belong to a church. I had been both warned and accused by some of my peers regarding not fishing in another man's pond, meaning stealing any of their members, which I honestly never would have wanted their infections. I strongly believe that the swapping of members is a root cause of the consistent negative issues across the board with many churches. Satan raises as much hell as he can in one house of God, and after that house has fallen, he simply moves on to the next. So again, in trying to separate NBC from the cycle of religious and traditional organizations, I created a two-sided flyer with one side displaying a picture of myself and my wife standing in front of the church building. This side of the flyer also displayed the church contact, service times, and address information as well as the churches logo and motto which read: **YOU ARE THE CHURCH, WE ARE THE MOVEMENT!**

On the second side of the flyer, we took a very nontraditional approach. Targeting the nonchurchgoers, I wanted to place these flyers in everyday places including local stores and supermarkets, hair salons, barbershops, and restaurants. If you've ever picked up one of these flyers from any of these locations, then you're familiar with the primary purpose of advertising such events as plays, concerts, comedy shows, and clubs. Knowing this, I created the second side of the flyer to look similar to these and draw attention. This side of the flyer read:

Boy did this go over well with some of the local pastors! Prior to these flyers coming out and the opening of the church, I never received even minimal words of encouragement or support from my peers. But once the flyers hit, these same peers congregated and plotted to destroy my name. They had to know that I wasn't truly planning on starting a club at church, even though that's what most of them had going on anyway. But to this day, I'm not sure if they were just jealous that they didn't think of the idea first or if they were upset because I was already targeting and tearing down their traditions!

With our first worship service at NBC, what I wanted to do was begin to lay the foundation of NBC. This foundation began by discussing who we are and what this New Body of Christ (NBC) stuff is all about. What are we talking about? When you walked through the doors of the church, you saw on the wall a large banner that displayed the church motto: **"You are the church!!! We are the movement!"** I knew some were wondering, what does that mean? I knew some people just heard that there was a new church and came just out of curiosity. We all know that folks are nosy! So some people that came to this first service only came to see who we were or even who all was there. People came to see if there was anything to it or again was this just another church? Was this just another fashion show? Was I just another pimp—excuse me, I meant pastor! Hey, I'm gon' keep it real again. We all know what folks say! But some people simply came to see was I just another pastor entertaining, showing off, singing. Others may have come to see how good and entertaining the choir or praise team would be, of which I had neither.

Some people came to see if it was just some more folks clubbing in church, you know dancing, the preacher whooping. In case you don't know what whooping is, whooping is a form of preaching and entertainment that originated in the black church, which includes heavy breathing, moaning, screaming, and singing at levels commonly heard only by pastors and heavy metal singers. Some came to see if I was just another pastor begging for money so that he can buy his suits and drive his Cadillac. I actually do drive a Cadillac, but let's clear that stereotype up, I work! I brought that truck before I was preaching! So don't let folks spread none of that mess about me being no pimp in the pulpit!

So what's this New Body of Christ all about? Well, right off the top, I began to kill many of the stereotypes. I began to separate and disassociate myself and NBC from what a lot of folks sadly enough have gotten familiar with or used to with churches! The first stereotype is the fashion show. For the first Sunday service at NBC, when the people arrived, they saw me standing up there in my T-shirt. Now the reason that me and some of the leadership as well were wearing the T-shirts was first because it was hot outside, and second,

I wanted to kill the whole church clothes history and tradition! There is no such thing as church clothes! When I had the flyers made for the start of NBC, I specifically put on the flyer, "No dress code. Come as you are!"

Now I know some people feel as if you should dress up to come to church (I'll deal with that in a minute). Some might have seen me up there and thought that because I'm not suited and booted that I didn't look like a pastor. My response to that is what does a pastor look like? Because I am a pastor! I am what God called me to be, whether I'm wearing this T-shirt or if I was fresh to death in my three piece-suit all the way down to my Stacy Adams! Fellas, y'all know some of y'all still got some Stacy Adams!

I wanted people to know that when they came to NBC, you could come as you are! Come in whatever it is that you have and know that there wouldn't be any smirks, evil looks, or funny faces staring; although I must admit that I'm pretty silly, so if you did come in wearing something crazy you might see me smiling at you, like, "Girl, you wearing them polka dots," or "Player, I see you in your mandarin suit!" But seriously, I had to kill this tradition from the start. Come as you are! Based on how I was feeling, some weeks I wore suits and some weeks when it was hot outside, hey, I'm sorry, but I wasn't about to burn up trying to impress anybody! The truth of the matter is that some folks don't have any church clothes! And again, what are church clothes? Church clothes are what your mama used to tell you to take off before you went outside to play because if you messed them up you knew what was going to happen!

The next thing that I had to murder, the next thing I had to lay to rest, was the perception that the pastor should entertain you. **I was not there to entertain you!** I apologize, I'm sorry. I'm on an assignment from God! God has a calling on my life and that calling was not to entertain you, so if you want entertainment, if entertainment is what you are looking for, I encourage you to find that! There are many concerts and festivals that I am sure are going on, and I wholeheartedly encourage you to buy a ticket! I don't sing, and although I think I can, my wife for some reason who I think is hating on me, insists on telling me that I can't sing! I also don't do the footwork, for those of you that have ever seen a preacher go off into his dance. I don't have my holy juke down to a groove.

Now I know I'm really about to make somebody mad, but if you are the type of person that feels like the pastor hasn't preached to you unless he whoops and hollers at you, then let me apologize beforehand for not preaching...TO YOU! Again, I am on assignment from God, and that is not my assignment! That's not what God called me to do! I am not here to entertain you! All that whooping and hollering, getting it in, look, if whooping and hollering at people actually worked, if whooping and hollering could get them demons out of some of these so-called church folks; if it could stop some of these attacks from the enemy that folks is really struggling with EVERY DAY, then there really wouldn't be any need for NBC. There would be no need for God to have called me, yet another pastor! Churches all over the world would be full. People all over the world would be saved! But to keep it real, folks out here with REAL problems, and by real I'm talking about the ones that are battling with some real strongholds, some real trials and tribulations, folks that are really trying to change their life, their predicament, or their situation. These folks are tired of that!

I'm sure you've heard or had this conversation before: "Girl, we had church today. Pastor showed out!" "He whooped and hollered all up and down that church!" That's crazy! Pastors have made a name for themselves based on their whooping and hollering and not the content of their message! You actually will hear people talking about pastor so and so is a bad boy! Why? Because he can breathe and talk like Darth Vader or Chewbacca all over the microphone in the pulpit? What does that accomplish? There's no power in that! Honestly, Satan is having a ball with that! Truth be told, some of these preachers and pastors are so good at whooping and hollering because that's all they are used to doing while Satan is busy whipping them all week! Anybody that has kids, and you know when you got to touch them up or if you can remember when you were a kid, like when I was a kid and I would get to the point where like the old folks used to say, "I was smelling myself." I'd be done got in some trouble or some mess where I earned a good touch-up! And my mama (yeah,

I'm telling Ma). Boy, I could whoop and holler! AHHH! PLEASE! No, MAMA! JESUS! HELP! I hope I haven't offended anybody!

"The pastor is writing about how he whips his kids!" YES, I DO! It's a lot of other folks that need to whip their kids too! People was mad when they heard about Pastor Creflo dollar in the news. Pastor Creflo didn't do anything wrong! Some of these kids nowadays are to the point where they have no fear! I'm gon' keep it real at NBC! We are a Bible church, and in case you didn't know that it was in your Bible! Proverbs 13:24 says that he who spares the rod hates his son, but he who loves him is careful to discipline him. So as we often hear, it doesn't say "spare the rod spoil the child," but whoever paraphrased it they were close enough!

"Withhold not correction from the child: for if thou beatest him with the rod, he shall not die. Thou shalt beat him with the rod, and shalt deliver his soul from hell" (Proverbs 23:13–14).

If you don't discipline your children, if you don't put any fear— and when I say fear, I mean fear in the sense of reverence—in your kids, then that's why little Suzie and Johny be cussing you out and they are only ten years old! If they cuss you out, what do you expect that the teacher can do with them? And we know what the police gon' do when they get them! So I don't care what the world says, God told us to be in this world but not of this world! That means we should do things differently than the world! The Bible says the LORD disciplines those he loves, as a father the son he delights in. I get my son the same way that God gets me sometimes because he loves me! He wants to keep me from some things. He wants to detour me from some places as well as some people! Amen. Don't despise the Lord's discipline church! Don't resent his rebuke!

But back to the whooping and hollering, like I was saying, that's why some of these pastors be hollering so much because it's become natural. They've become far too familiar with taking a beating! I find it a shame that "church folks" have gotten to the point that we like this! We've gotten to the point that we say and believe that this is church. WE HAD CHURCH TODAY! No, again, YOU ARE THE CHURCH!

I'm not lying, people! Some of you have heard folks ask about pastors. What do they ask? Can he pull it? Did he whoop and holler?

It's enough whooping and hollering going on! Too many mamas are hollering because they are losing their babies out here in these streets every day! Some of you have been hollering all week because it's just been one thing after another going on, one attack after another! It's Sunday, you down to your last twenty dollars until next Friday. You just got a final notice that your lights are about to get cut off! You are late on your rent! You just got an eviction notice! You can't find a job! You don't know how you are going to pay your bills! You don't know how you are going to pay for your child's daycare or summer program! You can't afford the medication that you need! Your baby mama or baby daddy are acting crazy! Child support is tripping! You stressing because your kids are acting a fool out here in the streets! You just got the results from your last appointment at the doctor's office! You're tired, you've reached your limit, and if just one more thing happens, you feel as if you are just going to SCREAM!

Screaming and hollering are natural responses whenever you are getting whipped! You don't need anybody to teach you how to scream! How about teaching me how to walk in victory and not defeat? Give me a word that's going to break this yoke, this curse, this stronghold in my life! Teach me how to get this devil up off me! I need a word from God to help me with some of this stuff that I'm fighting with!

I am not a pastor who is here to entertain you! If you want to hear singing, go to a concert; I hear New Edition is on tour! If you want whooping and hollering, there are several pastors doing it! But we are going to come together in fellowship and unity. We gon' gather in this house and touch and agree and lift up the most high God with thanksgiving in our hearts, with worship and praise. I'm gon' preach the Word of God to you for edification of the true church, the body of Christ, which by now you should know is you! I'm going to give you a word that challenges you, that encourages you, that motivates you. I'm going to give you a word that disturbs your spirit and pushes you to new levels. I will teach you who God is and help you find his purpose for your life, and together, we will be about the movement of God! Amen. So like I said, on the first day, I just wanted to lay the foundation! I didn't want to lose anybody, so my style of preaching was always to KISS you. In case you've never heard that term KISS before, it's an acronym that stands for "Keep it simple, stupid"!

Is it okay if I KISS you? Not because I believe or I'm saying that any of you are stupid. No, don't get offended, it's me. I just like simple stuff, so I'll be stupid! Somebody reading this say, "Go, stupid!" Boy, y'all is off the chain! Y'all alright with me!

God called me, and he knew who he was calling. That is who he wants me to be! I'm never going to get up here and ever try to be somebody else. I'm not Donnie McClurkin, so I will not be preaching and singing to you. I'm not Bishop Noel Jones, so I will not be flexing my vocabulary and intellect on you. I am wondrously created! God made me beautiful just like he made you. He called me to teach and preach the gospel, and so I'm going to do it just the way that God would have me to do it. Be you…that's when it's bea-u-tiful!

I am so thankful for the opportunity to spread the Gospel. I am so thankful that people from all over the world with different beliefs, backgrounds, and denominations will have the opportunity to read this book. It is my prayer that God would reveal himself to you as the supreme deity, as the way, the truth, and the life in Jesus's name. Amen.

I wanted to start this book of sermons with the first sermon I ever preached at New Body of Christ (NBC) Rockford, Illinois, a church in which I pastored and founded along with my wife, Natina, in June 2012. Just like many of you, I had been a member of multiple churches under different denominations where I experienced so many situations and occurrences, which I knew were not in line with God's will. It was the journeying through these valleys and dry places in which God revealed to me and I began to realize that the purpose and vision for the true bride and church of God had been lost. This first sermon discusses the "true church" as well as tears down many of the myths, stereotypes, and strongholds of many "church folks," as well as establishes and lays the foundation and vision, which God gave for his church and my purpose in starting NBC.

1

❖

New Body of Christ

> And I say also unto thee, That thou art Peter [the word *Peter* in Greek means rock] and upon this rock I will build my church; and the gates of hell shall not prevail against it. (Matthew 16:18 KJV)

> I am crucified with Christ: nevertheless, I live; yet not I, but Christ liveth in me: and the life which I now live in the flesh I live by the faith of the Son of God, who loved me, and gave himself for me. (Galatians 2:20 KJV)

If someone asked you or if you were to ask someone else the question, "Where do you attend church" or "What church do you belong to?" you would probably answer or you could expect to get such answers as Providence Baptist Church, St. Paul Church of God in Christ, Pentecostal Center, St. Mary's, Faith Walkers Assembly, or Faith Temple. Well, the name and vision that God gave me for his church which we would start was New Body of Christ (NBC). With that said, it is critical that we as Christians understand that it is not the name of the church that's most important but rather that we understand what the true church is. To explain, let's get into the text. It's good to have your Bibles to follow along. We will begin in the

Gospel of Matthew with the first referenced scripture from above, Matthew 16:18 which reads: *"And I say also unto thee, That thou art Peter* [the word *Peter* in Greek means rock] *and upon this rock I will build my church; and the gates of hell shall not prevail against it"* **(Matthew 16:18 KJV).**

The world along with Satan, the dark prince of this world, has taken the church and abused it! The word *abuse* simply means to misuse something. To take something that was created for one purpose or use and to misuse or use it for other uses or purposes. This is Satan's plan. This is his forte. This is what the enemy does. He is the great deceiver. The Bible says that Satan came to steal, kill, and destroy. So just like you, just like me, just like we were created for God's purpose and glory, Satan is trying to steal you from God! He's recruiting you! He's trying to steal the victory that Jesus Christ gave to all of us who are saved. In Satan's plan to accomplish this, he throws a collage of mess, confusion, and all sorts of deception and lies; wiles the Bible calls it. He throws these wiles at us with the hope and intent that we might turn away from God's path, purpose, and his plans for our lives. He does it in hopes that we might forfeit our victory and allow the enemy to take what God so wondrously created when he created man and use and abuse us for his purpose.

This plan of Satan's is the same for the church. To provide you with some background, in the passage from which our sermon scripture originates, Jesus was on the move as was customary for him. Jesus was going around teaching, preaching, and healing people of all sorts of diseases, sickness, and ailments. Jesus was traveling, and while he was traveling, he was recruiting and making disciples of men. Most importantly, Jesus was establishing relationships.

It's important that we understand that Jesus's ministry was never about starting a church in the sense of how the world views church. Jesus never had a nice building with pews and stained glass where he was the pastor and had an ushers and a mother's board, along with a mass choir or a praise team. Jesus didn't come to establish a church building and definitely not another religion. Religion is routine. Religion is anything that you practice, anything you do over and over. We religiously go to church (worldviews). We religiously go to work. Many people exercise or workout religiously. Look at this definition for *religion* as defined by Merriam-Webster: "A personal set or institutionalized system of religious attitudes, beliefs, and practices."

Have you ever been or maybe you know of a person that is in an institutionalized system? If so, then you probably know that most people don't like being institutionalized. This is what churches are doing. Church in a religious sense institutionalizes people! In efforts to control, churches are instilling members with whatever their religious attitudes, beliefs, and practices are. And as is the case with most institutions, should you dare to not fully conform, some form of punishment or condemnation follows. But the devil is a lie! It wasn't the purpose or ministry of Jesus, or rather, Jesus didn't come to institutionalize us! No, on the contrary, Jesus came to set us free! The Bible says that he who the son has set free is free indeed! So Jesus was never about setting up a church in the sense of a building or in the sense of religion, which has become the worldview of the church today. Contrary to many churches, which today are at a standstill, Jesus was always on the move! Jesus was the church! Wherever Jesus went, the crowds drew. The people would go to wherever Jesus was so that they could be healed! They would go so that they could be saved.

One of the focal points for our sermon scripture today is Simon Peter. Peter we know was one of the twelve disciples. As Jesus was going throughout the land, Galilee and Syria, again teaching and healing all kinds of sickness and disease, in the book of Matthew chapter 16, it reads:

> *When Jesus came into the coasts of Caesarea Philippi, he asked his disciples, saying, Whom do men say that I the Son of man am? And they said, Some say that thou art John the Baptist: some, Elias; and others, Jeremias, or one of the prophets. He saith unto them, But whom say ye that I am? Who do you say I am! And Simon Peter answered and said, Thou art the Christ, the Son of the living God. And Jesus answered and said unto him, Blessed art thou,*

Simon Barjona (Son of John): for flesh and blood hath not revealed it unto thee, but my Father which is in heaven. (Matthew 16:13–17 KJV)

Let's stop right there. When I look back over my life, and some of you should be able to witness to this as well, I remember being a child and going to church way back in the day when my mom would send me to Berean Baptist Church on the church bus, which used to ride through the neighborhood picking up kids. Some of you may have rode the church bus as well, or you can remember going to Sunday school. As a child, I was taught the good news of the Gospel. But even though this had been taught to me, even though it had been told to me and I was around it, it really wasn't clear. I really didn't have a revelation, a true understanding. Though flesh and blood had revealed it to me, and even though God knew and predestined who I was, I didn't have the full revelation or the relationship with Jesus that I would later come to have once I became a man. As the scripture says:

When I was a child, I spake as a child, I understood as a child, I thought as a child: but when I became a man, I put away childish things. (1 Corinthians 13:11 KJV)

It's good to bring your kids to church, and it was good that my mother had taught me at a young age. Because at least when I got older and I found myself in some trouble, or when I found myself in a situation where Mama or Daddy really couldn't help me, I knew where to turn. See, I got a friend of mine and even today he's a grown man well in his forties, and he knows who Jesus is but it hasn't fully been revealed. I was speaking to him one day, and he said that he really had never been through anything of great tribulation, and so if you've really never been through anything where there was nobody else that could help you, not mama, not daddy, not big mama; if you've never been down and out where you've cried so much that you

4

ran out of tears; if you've never thought about or felt like giving up; if life has never knocked you down, and you just felt like laying down for the count, then it hasn't fully been revealed to you who Jesus REALLY is and why he came! If you've never been sick to the point that the doctors didn't have the cure and had given up, then you might not know that Jesus is a healer! If you've never had something happen that just turned your world completely upside down and everybody was just waiting for you to go crazy and wondering how it was that you were still standing, and still maintaining, then you might not know that Jesus is a keeper!

See back then, it was my mother who was responsible, just like today if you don't know Christ then I'm responsible for teaching you about Jesus and who he is, but it's our Father which art in heaven that will reveal it to you! Let's go back to the text.

> **And I say also unto thee, That thou art Peter, and upon this rock I will build my church; and the gates of hell shall not prevail against it. (Matthew 16:18 KJV)**

As I've already stated, Jesus didn't come to build or establish a religion! The religious leaders, the Pharisees and the Sadducees in the Bible, they knew all about the Jewish laws, but what they didn't know was that the law couldn't save them! See the Pharisees and the Sadducees, they couldn't keep the laws and not only them, but neither can we! Because of sin, we were all cursed, found guilty, and sentenced to death! The Bible states:

> **For all have sinned, and come short of the glory of God. (Romans 3:23 KJV)**

This is the reason why Jesus had to come and save us from the law! We were slaves bound by the law! It was Jesus who paid our ransom at Calvary! It was Jesus who, through his crucifixion and resurrection, gave us the victory. Praise God! It is the enemy who, even after suffering this eternal loss, has not accepted defeat and still seeks to destroy God's plan of salvation. See, after Calvary, the disciples they went about attempting to do what Jesus had commissioned them to do. Jesus had given them the great commission, which is what we adopted as the mission statement of NBC and this movement. There is no reinventing of the wheel here. I see some of these churches, and they have these grand mission statements; but I often wonder, how can you do more than what Jesus told you to do? Jesus commissioned the disciples saying to them:

> ***Go ye therefore and teach all nations, baptizing them in the name of the father, and of the son, and of the Holy Ghost: Teaching them to observe all things whatsoever I have commanded you: and, lo, I am with you always, even unto the end of the world. Amen.* (Matthew 28:19–20 KJV)**

This was Jesus's mission statement! This was the movement! And this is what the disciples set out to do.

But how many of you know how much Satan hates a plan? He hates to see a plan come together. Oh, how Satan attempts to be the plan destroyer! So the disciples in doing what Jesus had commissioned them to do, and even though they had been with Jesus, even though Jesus had laid down his life at Calvary, even though he died so that we might live and even though on the third day he rose with all power, even though it's through Jesus that we have the victory, still Satan didn't give up! You should know that Satan doesn't give up! He's the epitome of persistence.

It was in the wilderness with Jesus that Satan tried to deceive Jesus and stop God's plan for our salvation! That didn't work, and so the Bible says that he left. So we see that he will leave, but you best believe that he will be back! He will not give up! He will try and find another way to stop God's plans for your life! If he can't get to you, he will go through those that are closest to you. He will go through your wife or your husband. He will attack your marriage! If your marriage is secure, he will try to go through your children. He will get your kids to act a fool! If that doesn't work, he will try to attack your finances! If that doesn't work, he will attack your health. He will find a way to cause some chaos and confusion in your life! He is the author of confusion, an adversary contrary to our God who is not a God of confusion!

So the disciples with both victory and the gift of the Holy Spirit went forward with the commission and movement of Christ, the true church that Jesus was building! They went forward teaching and preaching the Gospel of Christ and baptizing in the name of the Father and of the son and of the Holy Ghost. But Satan wasn't through then, and today he's still not through. Satan again went to work, and he began to devise yet another plan to divide the body of Christ, the true church! Satan went about establishing religions and denominations, creating confusion, which is still in so many so-called churches today! It's confusion, it's Satan, there are devils right in the church! Remember the movie with Samuel Jackson, *Snakes on a Plane*? Well, there are literally snakes in the church! But Jesus spoke something, and in this passage, Jesus says that **"thou are Peter, Rock and on this Rock I will build my church" and the gates of hell he said shall not prevail against it!**

One day as I read this, I began to think that he couldn't have been talking about building his church within walls and on the corner or intersection of two streets. He couldn't have been talking about these many modern-day churches/social clubs that we see hell prevailing in every day! Anybody that's been in church for any period has seen some real demons! You've seen Satan raise some hell right in church! Have you ever been to a church business meeting? God couldn't have been talking about that church! Going back to the text, Jesus asked the disciples, **first**, who people were saying that he was, and **second**, who they say that he is? It was Peter who spoke up and told him, "You are Christ the son of the living God."

"Blessed art thou" was Jesus's response to Simon, *"for flesh and blood did not reveal this to you but my Father in heaven."*

It was the Father who revealed it to Peter. Once the father had revealed it to Peter, Jesus then spoke, saying, *"Thou art Peter, Rock."*

This is the rock. Peter is the rock! This is how the church would be built, upon the revelation of who Jesus Christ is.

> *For with the heart man believeth unto righteousness; and with the mouth confession is made unto salvation.* **(Romans 10:10 KJV)**

This is the plan of God for salvation! See, in order to believe, it takes faith! Faith comes by hearing and hearing by the Word of God. Once you have heard, God the Father has to reveal it to you! Your spirit then bears witness. But then watch what happens. Right after this, right after the revelation, right after God had revealed to Peter who Jesus was, right after Jesus tells Peter that he was blessed, right after he had spoken his will, his plan to build his church, he then goes on to tell the disciples God's plan, his will. This is something that the true church must again seek—God's will, not our will. Your church may want to be mega even though you have yet to master minor. Your church may want musicians and a praise team leader with a combined pay that exceeds the Gap band and is more than your church's rent or mortgage. All these things may sound appealing, but what is God's will? Just like Jesus, the true church must be about our Father's business!

Back to our passage, Jesus tells the disciples God's will. He tells them that he had to go to Jerusalem and that he would suffer death and be raised again on the third day. And Mathew 16 verse 22 says:

> *Then Peter took him, and began to rebuke him, saying, Be it far from thee, Lord: this shall not be unto thee. But he turned, and said unto Peter, Get thee behind me, Satan: thou art an offence unto me: for thou savourest not the things that be of God, but those that be of men.* **(Matthew 16:22–23 KJV)**

Wow! Peter, rock, the rock in which Jesus would build his church. Just that quick Jesus told him, *"Get thee behind me, Satan:*

thou art an offense unto me: For thou savourest not the things that be of God, but those of men!"

The NIV says it like this: *"You are a stumbling block to me; you do not have in mind the concerns of God, but merely human concerns."*

Right here the Lord has spoken! Right here I present to you the problem with the church! Jesus is saying to Peter, to the church, you do not have in mind the concerns of God but merely human concerns! Did you see what she wore today? Who's preaching this week? Who's singing this week? When is ushers' annual day? When is men's day? When is women's day? Who's coming for the church anniversary this year? Again, did pastor pull it? Did he whoop?

Just as quickly as Satan got into Peter, Satan has gotten into the church! The church has become a stumbling block to Jesus. Too many people are getting hurt. Too many people are being misused in the church. Too many people experience hatred and not love.

This is the church that people no longer want to be a part of! This is the church that you can't get anybody to go to! All of us know somebody, there are many people that don't go, that won't come to your or any church. And we wonder why. It's this church that has no ministry. It's this church that has no love. As a matter of fact, forget about love, people don't even like each other! In this church, you'll find people sitting on the same pew, on one end talking about somebody on the opposite end. There's no love, there's no unity; it's only religion! Many of us have been members of different congregations in recent years past because we've been searching, better yet, seeking what it is that our heart's desire. Seeking to find your purpose, to serve and glorify God. Seeking to change our lives and to reach new levels! Seeking to walk into your destiny!

The other half of us were not much better. We know that the place that we call church couldn't be church. Not the church that Jesus was building! We know it's a mess! We know what's going on. We just keep going because we either feel like or Satan has convinced us that all churches are the same! All churches have problems! He's convinced us that all churches have confusion, and so we now just ignore the snakes in the church! We ignore the skunks even though common sense tells you that when you see a skunk you know at any moment it's capable of spraying, and whenever it does, you know that it's going to cause a problem! Snakes and skunks, might be the pastor, might be the deacons, and it might even be you! Yet we ignore everything going on both around and within us, and we tell ourselves that God will take care of it! And you know what, he will, but then again, maybe he won't?

A lot of times in life we sit around waiting on God, failing to realize that God has already given us everything that we need to succeed. But we stay committed to things that only hinder us. We stay committed to things like buildings. We stay committed to being charter members. We stay committed to where our mamas or daddies used to attend. We stay committed to where we were married or where we had loved ones' funerals. Satan gives us reason after reason to stay still, to stay in darkness, which is where he desires to keep us until we die. We stay still when we really should be a movement! The Bible tells us:

> **And have no fellowship with the unfruit-**
> **ful works of darkness, but rather reprove them.**
> **(Ephesians 5:11 KJV)**

Correct them! Why would anyone stay in fellowship with darkness? Why would anyone stay committed or connected to monuments! A monument is going nowhere! A monument is something erected in memory of a person or event, such as a building, pillar, or statue, for example *the Washington Monument.* The church is not a monument! The church is a movement.

A movement by definition is a series of organized activities working toward an objective. A movement is an organized effort to promote or attain an end, such as was with the civil rights movement. A movement consists of actions or activities as of a person or body of persons. A movement is a tactical or strategic shifting of a military unit.

Again, the motto of NBC is, "You are the church! We are the movement!"

For a multitude of reasons, people aren't coming to church. But the kingdom of God lives in us! The Word of God tells us that we are the salt of the earth to make it tolerable. We are the light of the world, a city set on a hill that cannot be hidden. The grand commission of God as I already said was to go ye therefore…Go is an action word. Go means to move! It is our commission to go out into these streets, into our neighborhoods and communities, into our city! Every Christian is an ambassador for the kingdom! You represent the kingdom! You speak for God! You have been commissioned, you have been anointed to go out and spread the good news! It's not enough to just invite people to your building and then feel like you've done your job! You are the new body of Christ, Jesus said better works shall you do! Jesus started his ministry at the age of thirty-two. He never set up a church, he was the church! He was the movement. In just three years, look at what he accomplished! A plan of salvation for the world! In three years, look at the many miracles he performed! The many people he healed! The demons he cast out! Jesus said, "Greater works shall you do!" Everybody is not going to come to your church building! Everybody don't want to hear your pastor! Everyone won't care for your choir! But right where you stand, right where you cross paths with people, you can take them to church right there! You can lead them to Christ, you can save them right there!

Christ loves the church! He gave himself for the church that he might sanctify and cleanse it, that he might present it to himself as a glorious church. Christ is coming back for his church without a spot wrinkle or blemish. You are that church! You, the baptized body of believers, the church was built upon you! Every time the Father reveals to another individual the body of Christ, the church grows!

Listen! Just as Jesus Christ lost his life for our sake! Just as he died, just as he laid down his life that we might live, still in the Gospel of Matthew chapter 16 in verses 24–25:

> ***Then said Jesus unto his disciples, If any man will come after me, let him deny himself, and take up his cross, and follow me. For whosoever will save his life shall lose it: and who-***

soever will lose his life for my sake shall find it.
(Matthew 16:24–25 KJV)

This leads us to our second sermon scripture for this message. Galatians 2:20, our vision statement at NBC reads,

I am crucified with Christ: nevertheless, I live; yet not I, but Christ liveth in me: and the life which I now live in the flesh I live by the faith of the Son of God, who loved me, and gave himself for me. **(Galatians 2:20 KJV)**

That's our vision, to die! We must die in our flesh, be crucified with Christ! We must lose our life for Christ's sake in order that we might find life! In order to be born again. In the Bible, Nicodemus had a hard time understanding this. Nicodemus was a Pharisee; he was one of the Jewish leaders. Jesus told Nicodemus, **"Except a man be born again, he cannot see the kingdom of God" (John 3:3 KJV).** Nicodemus asked, **"How can a man be born when he is old? Can he enter the second time into his mother's womb, and be born?" (John3:4 KJV).** How can these things be? See, Nicodemus heard, but the Father hadn't revealed it to Nicodemus. You are the church! The whole body of Christian believers.

As I said in the introduction, it doesn't matter where you came from, it doesn't matter your race, your sex, it doesn't matter your upbringing. It doesn't matter your struggles, your education, your occupation, your title; God is not a respecter of persons. It doesn't even matter the decisions you've made in your life up to this point, your mistakes and regrets, God's grace is sufficient! The blood of our Lord and Savior Jesus Christ, it covers it all! God still has a purpose and a plan for your life! He's granted you this day, this opportunity, so that you can become a part of the body of Christ! Today, you can become the true church.

In the book of 1 Corinthians chapter 12, I encourage you to read it, the Bible talks about the body of Christ and how the body is made up of many members just as our body is. We've got two arms and two legs, and we have both hands and feet, as well as two eyes. But it says that each member of our body still makes up only one body. Even more important if a person is missing some parts. Ask a lame man with no hands how important his feet are to his body. Ask a lame man with no feet or legs how important his hands are. Some of you may have broken bones in your body before. Think of how you felt or how hard it was when just one of your arms or legs was incapacitated in a cast or a sling for just a short period of time. Think of how important you realized that each member of your body is! How important it is to be whole! So it is with the church, the body of Christ!

As God has chosen us and chosen us for such a time as this, to go ye therefore, as God has gathered us on this earth as diverse as we are, we are all the body of Christ. As the song says:

> *I need you, you need me!*
> *Were all a part of God's body*
> *Stand with me. Agree with me*
> *Were all a part of God's body*
> *It is his will that every need be supplied*
> *You are important to me I need you to survive!*

As we serve the Most High together, always remember that you are the church and together we are the movement!

This is how God gave me this. Jesus said that you are Peter Rock, and on this rock I will build my church. You are the church! A baptized body of believers! That's the church. We need each other to survive. There is strength in unity! I was watching *Rise of the Planet of the Apes* the other day, and if you have ever seen the movie, recall what the Bible says about stick, and what Caesar the ape told the other ape. Caesar was uniting the apes, and there was one ape named Rocket that Caesar really didn't care for, but still when he was trying to unite the apes, he showed Rocket the same love. Well, another ape asked Caesar why he did this, and so to illustrate, Caesar took some sticks and he broke them alone and said, "Apes alone weak." We've probably all been broken at some point. We've all been weak!

None of us are perfect! None is better than the other. But after Caesar broke the sticks, he put all the broken sticks together and the sticks, even though they had once been broken, together they became much harder to break in which Caesar said to the elder ape, "Apes together strong!" We are those broken sticks! And even though we've all been broken, there is still strength in unity! United we stand, divided we fall!

That's what Satan has been doing to the world's church; he's been dividing it. Old against the young, deacons against the pastor, pastors against the deacons, everyone arguing, everyone focusing on things not of God. That's the church that Jesus rebuked Peter for becoming. So we are the church, the baptized body of believers; even individually, I'm a church, you are a church! Wherever I go, I take the kingdom with me! When you are the church, when you're a part of the movement, wherever you go, the kingdom goes. Go ye therefore! When you go, you're going to encounter people, people that don't know the Lord, people that are not saved. People living in darkness. That's when you must be the church, you have to be that light! All of us have been given gifts, strengths. Everyone reading this today is gifted to do something! God has given you this gift for his glory. God has a special calling on your life, a purpose. If you don't know what your gift or purpose is yet, don't worry, it is my ministry to get you to that knowledge and understanding. But individually, we all have gifts. Strengths that the Bible says that one of us can send one thousand demons to flight, but when we get together, something miraculous happens where strength multiplies to the extent where if one us can send one thousand, the Bibles says that two can send, not two thousand but ten thousand! That's multiplication! That's power! See when we get together, all on one accord, all working together toward the same purpose, now you have a movement! You are the church! We are the movement!

I like to watch movies as you'll learn about me. This power, this movement which I'm explaining, I see it like the Transformers! If you've ever seen the Transformers, they all had some unique individual strengths and powers, things they could transform into. But sometimes what would happen is that sometimes they would come up against some stuff! Sometimes they would encounter some problems! I pray someone gets this! Sometimes they would be up against some stuff, some Decepticons, that was much bigger and stronger than them. Sometimes they were fighting some stuff that alone they just couldn't seem to handle. Have you ever felt like sometimes it's just some stuff that you encounter, some stuff that you go through, and you just don't know what to do! It's in these situations you have to be careful with who you call because how many of you know that you just can't call on anybody. Naw, see some folks just don't quite fit into God's plan for your life. Some folks you call, and they just gon' make the situation worse! If you are struggling with being delivered from drugs and you are fighting that demon, but one night it gets rough, and you feel like a lil taste, you can't call your homies you used to get high with, because you just got delivered, and they still waiting on they deliverance! Yeah, you swore you were full, and you had finished your last taste. But they are over there, and they are still waiting for their next delivery! **You can't call them! They don't fit God's plan for your life!**

Have you ever heard the saying, don't tell nobody your problems that ain't qualified to help? You can't call everybody! See, some folks calling Muhammad and Allah. Some folks are calling on the Virgin Mary and a bunch of other saints! My advice is that you better call the name above all names! You better call the way, the truth, and the life! You better call the only way to get to the father, you better call on **JESUS**! Somebody say Jesus! When you call on the name of Jesus, a miracle takes place! When you call on the name of Jesus, something miraculous happens! I was talking about the Transformers, how they all got different gifts and powers, but sometimes they need even more power! That's when they join together, that's when they call on other members of the body. That's when they join together, and they form the movement! And today is your day! Today God had ordained for you. Today, as you have read this message, if God has revealed to you who Jesus Christ is, then today you are blessed.

"Blessed art thou for flesh and blood did not reveal this to you, but my Father in heaven."

Today, Jesus says to you that you are rock, and on this rock, he will build his church. Today is your day to become the church! Today is your opportunity to join the movement!

Say this prayer:

> *Heavenly Father, thank you for choosing me. Thank you for sanctifying me and appointing me as a prophet to the nations! Thank you for revealing to me who you are as well as your purpose for me and for your church. I pray that you use me, Lord, for your purpose and glory. I pray that you would anoint me for the same. Bless me to carry out your plans and your great commission. In Jesus's name, amen.*

2

David's Sermon

This sermon takes a look into the Old Testament, the book of 1 Samuel, which discusses events in the life of King David, one of my favorite figures in the Bible, a great fighter, a great ruler, and a great man of faith. At times in our lives, it's easy to lose sight. When facing trials and tribulations, we forget that God is still in control, and all things are working together for the good to them that love God, to them who are called according to his purpose. In looking at the life of David, we are able to see God's plans and remember that God has not forgotten about us.

In 1 Samuel 17, we find the story of David and Goliath, a story that most are familiar with. The story of how David the shepherd boy defeated Goliath the Giant with only his sling and a stone. In this sermon, I want to look into not only this encouraging and great story but also into the life of David and the events leading up to this pivotal episode of David and Goliath. I want to do this because I believe that in the life of David as well as the story of David and Goliath, there are some valuable life lessons that we can learn from David, again just a shepherd boy in charge of watching over his earthly father Jesse's cattle, but as we take a closer look at the life of David, we will also see God the Father and his plans, what he put David in charge of. We will see David's purpose and destiny to become the king of Israel. I encourage you to have your Bible handy, and I want to start at the beginning of 1 Samuel 17 so that we can get the background and understanding as to what was going on and what led to this pivotal episode in the life of David.

David and Goliath

Now the Philistines gathered their forces for war and assembled at Sokoh in Judah. They pitched camp at Ephes Dammim, between Sokoh and Azekah. Saul and the Israelites assembled and camped in the Valley of Elah and drew up their battle line to meet the Philistines. The Philistines occupied one hill and the Israelites another, with the valley between them. A champion named Goliath, who was from Gath, came out of the Philistine camp. His height was six cubits and a span.
(Which translates to nine feet nine inches! He was a biggin!)
He had a bronze helmet on his head and wore a coat of scale armor of bronze weighing five thousand shekels;
(Which is about 125lbs!)
on his legs he wore bronze greaves, and a bronze javelin was slung on his back. His spear shaft was like a weaver's rod, and its iron point weighed six hundred shekels. His shield bearer went ahead of him. Goliath stood and shouted to the ranks of Israel, "Why do you come out and line up for battle? Am I not a Philistine, and are you not the servants of Saul? Choose a man and have him come down to me. If he is able to fight and kill me, we will become your subjects; but if I overcome him and kill him, you will become our subjects and serve us." Then the Philistine said, "This day I defy the

armies of Israel! Give me a man and let us fight each other."

(Goliath was calling them out!)

On hearing the Philistine's words, Saul and all the Israelites were dismayed and terrified. (1 Samuel 17 NIV)

So let me stop right here for a minute, and let's do a pulse check! I'm wondering how many Sauls are reading this right now? Have you ever been like Saul? How many times and how many people have you allowed to dismay you? How many people have you allowed to slow you down, to stop you in your tracks, or even better to get you off track, off God's path. How many reports from the enemy, the doctor, the haters, have you believed? Who have you allowed to strike fear in your heart? Who have you allowed to paralyze you? Again verse 11 reads, **"On hearing the Philistine's words, Saul and all the Israelites were dismayed and terrified."**

Saul the King! Saul the leader of Israel and all of the Israelites! Not only Saul but also all the soldiers! At the words of Goliath, they were dismayed and terrified! If we were in church right now, I would tell you to look over at your neighbor and tell your neighbor, "Don't be scared!" Look at verses 12–15! Let's look at David.

Now David was the son of an Ephrathite named Jesse, who was from Bethlehem in Judah. Jesse had eight sons, Jesse's three oldest sons had followed Saul to the war: The first-born was Eliab; the second, Abinadab; and the third, Shammah. David was the youngest. The three oldest followed Saul, but David went back and forth from Saul to tend his father's sheep at Bethlehem.

Let's pause there for a second. As I wrote in the introduction, when we look at the life of David, we get a good look at God's purpose! We get a look at God's plan! I want to back up in the scriptures for just a little while to show you how God works. I want to show you how God is the alpha and the omega, the beginning and the end. I want to show you how God is that author and the creator of all things. In your life, there is a prophecy. God's plans for your life. Think of your life like a story, which has already been written much like a movie script. When we watch a movie or when we go to the movies, we don't know the full story. At the most, we may have seen previews, but we don't know what's going to happen. We don't know all the drama, suspense, action, or the many close calls waiting. When we go to the movie, and as we watch the movie, especially a good movie such as an action packed or a murder mystery movie, all these things catch us by surprise. These are the moments that have us on the edge of our seats. They have us holding our breath and cringing, even clinging to whoever is sitting next to us. We go through all these ups and downs as if we are riding on an emotional roller coaster. But the author, the one who wrote the story, along with the director and the producer, know the beginning as well as how the story is going to end. Nothing catches them by surprise!

I want to back up just to show you how God is in control of all things! I want to show you from the life of David how God works. How God created us all with a purpose and how God has a calling not only over David's life but also over your life! Just as Jeremiah the prophet prophesized the plans of God for his own life, God has plans for your life! Plans designed before you were formed in the womb. Plans to prosper you and not to harm you! Again, you were created with a purpose. You can read and study this later if you'd like to, but if you back up in the book of 1 Samuel, you'll find where God had rejected King Saul for disobeying his commandments and because of this God was going to take the kingdom of Israel away from Saul. The book of Proverbs says that the wealth of the wicked is laid up for the righteous. So not only was God going to take the kingdom of Israel away from Saul, but in his plan, God had already chosen a new king! Saul's time was up, his season was ending. God was about to do a new thing, much like he's doing with you! It's a new season, it's a new day, a fresh anointing is coming your way! That's why you have to be ready, always! You have to be prepared! You can't keep looking back to your past! You can't keep focusing on your struggles, your shortcomings, or even the people that did you wrong. No, you have to be in position, receiving position, for what God is about to do! If you believe it, say, "I BELIEVE!"

So in going back, if you were to look at 1 Samuel 16, you'll see where God told Samuel to stop mourning for Saul; I have rejected him. That's a word for somebody reading this. You're still mourning about something in your life! Something in your life that God meant for just a season, you keep trying to make it a lifetime. There are some people in your life that you know are no good for you, and you should have long let them go. Folks are holding you back! God is saying stop mourning over that for I have rejected it! God told Samuel take a vial of oil and go to Bethlehem and find a man named Jesse, for I have chosen one of his sons to be the new king. So Samuel did as he was instructed, and he went to Bethlehem. When he arrived in Bethlehem, the Bible records that he performed the purification rights on Jesse and his sons. When he saw the sons of Jesse, the Bible says that he took one look at Eliab and was sure that this was the man that God had chosen. He's not the only one! Just as we've all been Saul before, we've also all been Samuel. What am I saying? I'm glad that you asked! How many people, how many opportunities, how many doors in your life have you just been sure that this was it? You were sure that this was the one. Often in life just based off how good something looks on the outside, we assume, and we want it to be the one! But the Bible says that we walk by faith and not by sight! The Bible tells us that God's thoughts are not our thoughts, and his ways are not our ways! So when Samuel saw Eliab, based off how Eliab looked, he was sure that this was the man that God had chosen. But 1 Samuel 16:7 says:

> **But the LORD said to Samuel, "Do not look at his appearance or at his physical stature, because I have refused him. For *the LORD does* not *see* as man sees; for man looks at the outward appearance, but the LORD looks at the heart." (1 Samuel 16:7 NKJV)**

Somebody needs to thank God for that! Matter of fact, we all should praise God for that! At one time in your life, you might have gotten by just based off your looks. You might have got the hook up, you might have got in the club, you might have got a free sandwich or fries included with your order at McDonalds. At one time in your life, you might have gotten what you wanted just based on how good you look. I know some of us still think we look good! You still think that you still got it! But I got some news for you, as good as you look even today, none of us look like we used to! So I am thankful, I praise God for looking at the heart! So God told Samuel, "No, that's not him." So Jesse told another of his sons, Abinadab, to come and again God said, "No, that's not him either." Then Jesse called a third son, Shamman, and again God said, "No, that's not him." Eight sons in total! This was done with all seven of his sons. Samuel said the Lord has not chosen any of them, are there anymore? Declare this! Say out loud, what God has for me is for me! Say it again! What God has for me is for me! You don't have to worry about nobody taking it! You don't have to worry about being overlooked! You don't have to worry about being left out! Folks might look over you, folks might look at you and decide that you're not good enough! You're not tall enough. You're not built enough! You're not curvy enough! You're just not the one. But thank God that what God has for me it is for me! Samuel asked Jesse, "Are there any more sons?" Jesse replied, "Well, there is the youngest, but he is out there with the sheep." Again, because David was the shepherd boy, he was in the field. Now it might not sound like the best job. It's not a prestigious title. He wasn't a soldier like his brothers. But if it's one thing about David, he was faithful! He was faithful with the little that he had. This is what God wants from us. This is what God required that we do. Jesus said,

If you are faithful in little things, you will be faithful in large ones. But if you are dishonest in little things, you won't be honest with greater responsibilities. (Luke 16:10 NLT)

David was faithful! He was also where he was supposed to be. He was doing what he was supposed to do! He was working. He was in position. I'm talking to you right now. David was in the field waiting like a waiter! "Send for him at once," Samuel said. "We will not sit down and eat until he arrives!" Have you ever heard the saying, the party ain't a party until I walk in! We used to say, "I'm the life of the party!" So Samuel sent for David, and when David shows up, God says, "This is him. Anoint him!"

Here is wisdom. Here is the lesson. When you're working, when you're waiting like a waiter, when you're in position doing the work that was entrusted to you to do no matter how major or minor that work may be, when you're where God has for you to be, that's when and where God can send for you! So David stood there in front of his brothers, and Samuel took that olive oil and poured it on David's head and the Bible says that the Spirit of the Lord came upon David and gave him power from that day on! God anoints you with power for ministry! He anoints you for your purpose, to do his works, and to glorify him! There is no need in anointing someone if they have nothing to do! There is no need in anointing someone if they are not going to do something. When you think about the makeup of the church, the true church, the body of Christ, In Ephesians 4:11–12, Paul says,

So Christ himself gave the apostles, the prophets, the evangelists, the pastors and teachers, to equip his people for works of service, so that the body of Christ may be built up. (Ephesians 4:11–12 NIV)

There is work to be done! The church has a purpose! And no, it's not just about fellowshipping, singing, dancing, and eating. It's not just about coming to church! We must become the church! The purpose of the church is to be a movement! The church should be alive! The church should be on the go! The church is not a monument! A monument is a statue or a structure placed by or over a grave in memory of the dead! But we serve a risen savior! Jesus is alive and so the church should be alive! God anoints us for ministry, whatever your ministry might be. If God called you to it, he'll bring you through it!

Let me get back to David. Alright, so in the life of David, listen to what happens next. Look at how God works! I want you to see how God is in control, again how He's already written the story and why we should trust and submit to his plans! Because as I've said many times before that nothing that we're planning could ever beat God's plans for our lives! So Samuel anoints David and then he leaves. Now I don't know about you, but when I read that, I found that a little odd. I found it a little odd because if somebody sent by God anoints you, then Jesus empowers you. I mean, many times we see in the Bible where Jesus healed people. We're able to see where either as soon as Jesus touched them or even just spoke a word, something miraculous happened right then! And come on that's what we want! We are a microwave generation! We want microwave blessings! Do it now, God! Come on you've seen it, as soon as we come to church, as soon as we join, as soon as we become saved, we want all our problems resolved right then, right now! But it's important for us to see that at this moment when Samuel anoints David, Samuel leaves! David doesn't become king, not in the physical, nor the flesh, not that day, nor at that moment. Early in my ministry at a time when I was becoming discouraged because things weren't happening for the ministry as I thought they should and so I was starting to question God, one of my mentors, Dr. Charles Washington, told me something that I'll never forget. He said to me, "You've been anointed but not appointed!" So Samuel anoints David and then he leaves. Saul is still the king. But God's plans for David, his plans to prosper him and not to harm him, his plans to give him hope and a future, it's all beginning to unfold. Again, just like in a movie, don't leave to go get your popcorn; now is not the time. The plot to the movie, if you will, is beginning to unfold! Saul is still the king, but the Bible records that the Spirit of the Lord, his anointing, had left Saul and an evil spirit from the Lord tormented him. Can you see God's plan? Can you see how God is working it out? Can you see how God is moving things not only in the life of David, but how He's also moving things in your life right now? I'm showing you the life of David that you might see how God's plan is working in your life! How His plan is starting to manifest! How it's already done!

An evil spirit was now tormenting Saul. God's anointing had left. Now pay close attention to what happens next. Some of Saul's aids suggested to Saul that he find a good harpist to play for him so that whenever the evil spirit from God came, the harpist could play and make him feel better. This is good! God is awesome! When we look at the life of David, something else that we can learn from David's life, the Word of God in the book of Proverbs 18:16 says,

A man's gift maketh room for him, and bringeth him before great men. (Proverbs 18:16 KJV)

So Saul tells his aids to find someone who plays well, and one of his aids replies,

I have seen a son of Jesse of Bethlehem who knows how to play the lyre. He is a brave man and a warrior. He speaks well and is a fine-looking man. And the LORD is with him. (1 Samuel 16:18 NIV)

All of David's life he had been overlooked! All of David's life he had been seen as the last of Jesse's sons! David went from last to first! He went from the last choice to the first choice! And why? Because the Lord was with him! Because of God's anointing! Greater is he that is in me than he that is in the world! So Saul sends for David, and David enters Saul's service; and right away, Saul likes David. David also becomes one of Saul's armor bearers. Again, I ask you, can you see God's plan at work? I want to show you this because again we're able to see in the life of David how God was always there. How God's plan was always working in the life of David. And even though others couldn't see it—including his father, his seven brothers and even Samuel—even though we couldn't see it, in the same way, God has always been working in our lives! Whatever the problem, whatever the situation, whatever the trials and tribulations, how God is ordering your steps!

> **The steps of a good man are ordered by the LORD: and he delighteth in his way. (Psalm 37:23 KJV)**

God was ordering David's steps! Not that David didn't have his share of trials and tribulations, his share of suffering and perseverance. You can read several of the Psalms of David and see all that he endured. Later in David's life, if you read in 1 Samuel 19, you'll see where David would have to flee from Saul as Saul became jealous of him both as a warrior whose popularity was spreading as well as knowing that God was with and had chosen David. Saul would even try to kill David. So even though David's steps were ordered by God, even though David was anointed, David still had to endure hardships. But again, if God brought you to it, he'll bring you through it!

But getting back to our passage for today in 1 Samuel 17, verse 16 reads, **"For forty days the Philistine came forward every morning and evening and took his stand."**

Calling Israel out! Tormenting them! Daring just one of them to come forward! Verses 17 to 25 reads:

> **Now Jesse said to his son David, "Take this ephah of roasted grain and these ten loaves of bread for your brothers and hurry to their camp. Take along these ten cheeses to the commander of their unit. See how your brothers are and bring back some assurance from them. They are with Saul and all the men of Israel in the Valley of Elah, fighting against the Philistines." Early in the morning David left the flock in the care of a shepherd, loaded up and set out, as Jesse had directed. He reached the camp as the army was going out to its battle positions, shouting the war cry. Israel and**

> the Philistines were drawing up their lines facing each other. David left his things with the keeper of supplies, ran to the battle lines and asked his brothers how they were. As he was talking with them, Goliath, the Philistine champion from Gath, stepped out from his lines and shouted his usual defiance, and David heard it. Whenever the Israelites saw the man, they all fled from him in great fear. Now the Israelites had been saying, "Do you see how this man keeps coming out? He comes out to defy Israel. The king will give great wealth to the man who kills him. He will also give him his daughter in marriage and will exempt his family from taxes in Israel."

Remember this: the reward comes after the test! The reward comes after the tribulation, after the struggle! No test, no testimony! See, when we go through something, when we go through our share of troubles, when we face obstacles in our lives, the first thing the enemy wants you to think is that you're being punished. The devil wants you to think that God has forgotten about you, that God has let you down. I want to tell you that it's not a letdown, it's a setup! Verses 26 to 28 reads:

> David asked the men standing near him, "What will be done for the man who kills this Philistine and removes this disgrace from Israel? Who is this uncircumcised Philistine that he should defy the armies of the living God?" They repeated to him what they had been saying and told him, "This is what will be done for the man who kills him." When Eliab, David's oldest brother, heard him speaking with the men, he burned with anger at him and asked, "Why have you come down here?"

I can just hear him. I can hear the haters! "Why are you here anyway, you don't belong here!"

And with whom did you leave those few sheep in the wilderness?

See, people always want to put you where they are comfortable with you at! You might as well get used to it! They did it to Jesus, "Awe, he ain't nobody, ain't that Mary's boy the carpenter." They did it to David, and I want to testify and let you know that they did it and are still doing it to me! Some people are only comfortable with you to a certain extent, to a certain level. As long as you are on their level, you're fine; but as soon as you get a little success, they are coming for you! David's brother said:

> **"Why have you come down here? I know how conceited you are and how wicked your heart is; you came down only to watch the battle." (1 Samuel 17:28 NIV)**

There will always be someone! For David, it was his brother; for you, it might be another family member or friend. There will always be somebody that tries to hold you back, and their primary motive is because they were too scared to do it. But again, I love David! There is so much that we can learn from David. Look at what David does! Again verses 28–29 reads:

> **"Why have you come down here? I know how conceited you are and how wicked your heart is; you came down only to watch the battle."**
>
> **"Now what have I done?" said David. "Can't I even speak?"**

But look at David, look at verse 30:

**He then turned away to someone else and
brought up the same matter.**

You might be on the right path, you might have the right vision, but on the path to your breakthrough, on the path to your destiny, you have to know when to turn! Left, right, off, on, you must learn how to turn away. From the people, from some stuff, from some bad habits, from some things that are weighing you down, from anything that might be holding you back! You have to turn away! It's a distraction! Satan is trying to distract you! Some people, all they are, are distractions! You have to know which fight to fight! David knew which fight to fight! Goliath was the enemy! Goliath was the giant! Goliath was the one who was standing in the way of the Israelites! Goliath was the one who was responsible for paralyzing God's children. Goliath was the one not only threatening but actually holding up, blocking the blessings of God's chosen ones! But no one would fight Goliath! I bet there were a lot of fights going on between the camp of the Israelites! You've seen it! Anybody that's been in church for just two weeks you've seen it. I can only imagine the fights going on in the camp!

"You're supposed to be the leader!"

"Any other time you want to be the shot caller, get your butt out there now!"

"Where all that gangsta talk now?"

"Look at him over there scared!"

"I ain't going 'cause I ain't the leader!"

"They don't pay me enough!"

All these other fights going on amongst the camp of Israel! This is how it is with us! This is how it is in our lives! Sadly, this is how it is in the church. We spend all our time and energy fighting each other, fighting the wrong fights when there's a real fight out there that we all need to be fighting together! It's some real stuff out there that's picking us off one by one, that's destroying our lives, that's stealing our joy and blessings daily! But don't nobody want to fight that fight!

Don't nobody want to fight the good fight! Nobody wants to face off with the giant, the real enemy! Some people feel better tearing down each other. It makes them feel like Goliath! It makes them feel like a giant! Here you have it David's brother, a soldier, fearful of Goliath but coming at David! Starting a fight with David because he was too scared to fight Goliath! It was a setup from Satan! It was Satan's attempt to distract David from his purpose and destiny, from what God had prepared and anointed him to do! But David teaches us something! David doesn't get distracted! David stays on track! He stays on purpose! Just as you need to do! Stay on purpose! David says you know what I'm not getting sidetracked! David says, "I'm not bothering with you! I'm not about to listen to somebody that can't help me! He's scared, how can he help me? He's never done what I'm about to do!" Some folks in your life you must do like David! You have to understand that they can't help you! Satan only put them there to distract you, to infect you! All they can do is hurt you! Some people you have to learn how to just turn away! You have to learn how to keep it moving! David kept it moving! Reading on in the passage verses 30 to 33 says:

> **He then turned away to someone else and brought up the same matter and the men answered him as before. What David said was overheard and reported to Saul, and Saul sent for him. David said to Saul, "Let no one lose heart on account of this Philistine; your servant will go and fight him." Saul replied, "You are not able to go out against this Philistine and fight him; you are only a young man, and he has been a warrior from his youth."**

There it is again, the king! Because he was too scared, because he wasn't going to do it, all he could do was infect David! All he could do was give David what he had! But David did not let that stop him! David didn't allow Saul to infect him! David knew who he was!

I've said it before, you gotta know what you know! David knew what he knew! Verses 34 to 37:

> **But David said to Saul, "Your servant has been keeping his father's sheep. When a lion or a bear came and carried off a sheep from the flock, I went after it, struck it and rescued the sheep from its mouth. When it turned on me, I seized it by its hair, struck it and killed it. Your servant has killed both the lion and the bear; this uncircumcised Philistine will be like one of them, because he has defied the armies of the living God. The LORD who rescued me from the paw of the lion and the paw of the bear will rescue me from the hand of this Philistine."**

David said this ain't nothing! David said, "I'm built for this!" Gone, David! David was a man of faith! Through faith, nothing is impossible, and all things are possible! Even the word itself, *impossible* says, I'M POSSIBLE! Are there any Davids reading this? Is there anybody reading this that God has ever brought you through something? Is there anybody who can testify like David that the enemy thought he had me? The same God that brought you through that, he can bring you through this! Whatever you might be going through, He has plans to bring you through it! It's already done! In Jesus's name, it's already done! Cast all your cares upon him for he cares for you!

> **Come to me, all you who are weary and burdened, and I will give you rest. Take my yoke upon you and learn from me, For I am gentle and humble in heart, and you will find rest for your souls. For my yoke is easy and my burden is light! (Matthew 11:28–30 NIV)**

It's already done! All you have to do is get your David on! Fear not!

> **Do not be afraid. Stand firm and you will see the deliverance the LORD will bring you today. The Egyptians you see today you will never see again. The LORD will fight for you; you need only to be still. (Exodus 14:13–14 NIV)**

Now I don't know if David convinced or inspired Saul! I don't know if Saul believed that David could do it, but Saul surely knew that he wasn't going to do it! First Samuel 17:37b reads:

> **Saul said to David, "Go, and the LORD be with you."**

Verses 38 to 39 say,

> **Then Saul dressed David in his own tunic. He put a coat of armor on him and a bronze helmet on his head. David fastened on his sword over the tunic and tried walking around, because he was not used to them.**

Saul tried to dress David! Saul tried to give David his armor! What he would use I guess if he wasn't too scared to fight Goliath! But you have to be careful what you allow other people to dress you in! You have to be careful what you allow folks to put on you! Don't ever let anyone give you something that didn't work for them! People will try to give you their opinions. People will try to give you advice about your marriage, your relationship, your children, and even your finances! And they might even mean good, but remember all help isn't good help! Verse 39 continued…

> **"I cannot go in these," he said to Saul, "because I am not used to them." So he took them off.**

I have a question for you. What are you used to? What are you used to, and is it working for you? When you find yourself facing an obstacle or a challenge, when it's time for battle, what are you used to? Are you used to running like the army of Israel? Are you used to worrying? Are you used to arguing with folks and fighting with words? Are you used to calling certain people whenever you go through something? Are you used to turning to drugs or alcohol? What are you used to, and how is it working for you? What do you use to fight off the attacks of the enemy?

> **David said "I cannot go in these," because I am not used to them."**

Verse 39 continued:

> **So he took them off. Then he took his staff in his hand, chose five smooth stones from the stream, put them in the pouch of his shepherd's bag and, with his sling in his hand, approached the Philistine.**

It doesn't take much! With God on your side, it doesn't take much! Victory is mine! You already have the victory! Jesus said, "Truly I tell you that if you have faith the size of a mustard seed you can move a mountain"! Verses 41 to 47 reads:

> **Meanwhile, the Philistine, with his shield bearer in front of him, kept coming closer to David. He looked David over and saw that he was little more than a boy, glowing with health and handsome, and he despised him. He said to David, "Am I a dog, that you come at me with sticks?" And the Philistine cursed David by his gods. "Come here," he said, "and I'll give your flesh to the birds and the wild animals!" David said to the Philistine, "You come**

> **against me with sword and spear and javelin, but I come against you in the name of the LORD Almighty, the God of the armies of Israel, whom you have defied. This day the LORD will deliver you into my hands, and I'll strike you down and cut off your head. This very day I will give the carcasses of the Philistine army to the birds and the wild animals, and the whole world will know that there is a God in Israel. All those gathered here will know that it is not by sword or spear that the LORD saves; for the battle is the LORD's, and he will give all of you into our hands."**

Somebody reading this you need to tell the enemy just like David! Whatever you are battling with, whoever or whatever it is that is telling you that they got you and what they are going to do to you, tell it like David:

> **You come against me with (WHATEVER IT IS), but I come against you in the name of the LORD Almighty. This day the LORD will deliver you into my hands, and I'll strike you down and cut off your head.**

In the story of David and Goliath, Goliath was the enemy. Goliath had a reputation. He had defeated and slayed many! He was official; we can check his track record just like Satan's. In our story, Satan is the enemy. He's real! He has sent many folks off! He has stolen many blessings! He has taken many lives! But you must remember David! You must be like David! David knew what he knew! David had faith even when no one else did. David believed! David wasn't faking, David wasn't fronting. Unlike all the army of Israel, including David's brothers, David wasn't just wearing the uniform. David was prepared! David was ready! David mastered what his job was, shepherding. He mastered what his gift was as well as his weapon.

David had been overlooked! He wanted to join Saul's army before, but David had been denied promotion because he was not believed to have what the others had. He was too small, too young. But David had something that no one else had, not even in the so-called position of soldier! No one who wore the title, no one who got the pay! Y'all don't feel me! It's a lot of folks out here moonlighting, coasting, wearing titles in positions but not doing the work! They are simply wearing the uniform! Their only concern is to look good in their uniform! A lot of church folks, a lot of Christians, they may look good in their suits! They look good in their church clothes. They look like other people think they should look in the same way that many folks think that a pastor or a first lady or any Christian should look. They look good in their security uniform with their flashlights in their hand, but that's all there is to them. They have no weapons; they're just flashlight cops. I SEE YOU, topflight security like Craig and Dayday, they are not the real thing! But David was real! David was fearless! David had been anointed and had the Spirit and power of God!

For God has not given us a spirit of fear, but of power and of love and of a sound mind!! (2 Timothy 1:7 KJV)

So yes, we know that Goliath was a giant that stood over nine feet tall and was facing off against all of Israel but still he was no threat for the Lord. Just like whatever you might be facing now know that:

Greater is he that is in you than he that is in the world. (1 John 4:4 KJV)

Know that:

No weapon formed against you shall prosper. (Isaiah 54:17)

It was David who said in the book of Psalms:

A thousand may fall at your side and ten thousands at your right hand but it will not come near you. (Psalm 91:7 NIV)

David shows us how to conquer the enemy! David shows us how to fight! Verses 48–50 reads:

As the Philistine moved closer to attack him, David ran quickly toward the battle line to meet him. Reaching into his bag and taking out a stone, he slung it and struck the Philistine on the forehead. The stone sank into his forehead, and he fell facedown on the ground. So David triumphed over the Philistine with a sling and a stone.

Remember with God on your side it won't take much! Verses 50 to 54 continued:

Without a sword in his hand he struck down the Philistine and killed him. David ran and stood over him. He took hold of the Philistine's sword and drew it from the sheath. After he killed him, he cut off his head with the sword. When the Philistines saw that their hero was dead, they turned and ran. Then the men of Israel and Judah surged forward with a shout and pursued the Philistines to the entrance of Gath and to the gates of Ekron. Their dead were strewn along the Shaaraim road to Gath and Ekron. When the Israelites returned from chasing the Philistines, they plundered their camp. David took the Philistine's head and

brought it to Jerusalem; he put the Philistine's weapons in his own tent.

David conquered and killed Goliath the Giant! It's time for you to kill yours! Giants do die; the bigger they are, the harder they fall! You just have to stand up to your giants! You have to carry your cross! You must overcome your obstacles in order to reach your destiny, in order to get the victory! Otherwise just like the Army of Israel, you'll stay right where you are, whether it be for forty days or forty years they stayed scared, and they stayed still because fear will paralyze you! Goliath taunted them for forty days straight! How long has Satan been taunting you? How long have you been facing off with Satan? You muster up a little courage, a little faith, a little energy. You get a word, you get some encouragement, you decide that this is the last time, the last day, the last year that you're going to go through or struggle with this. You make up your mind to do something. I'm going back to school, I'm going to start looking for another job, I'm going to change my life, I'm going to change my career, I'm going to finish what I started, I'm going to write this book, I'm going to get my situation in order! Just like the army of Israel, you show up and you face off, but as soon as Goliath, as soon as the giant shows himself, as soon as the enemy appears, you run. The Bible says,

Be sober, be vigilant; because your adversary the devil as a roaring lion walks to and fro seeking whom he may devour. (1 Peter 5:8 KJV)

And so, every time he says something or every time you hear some bad news, as soon as he challenges you just like the army of Israel, you run again. Well, today is your day to stop running! Today is the day that you get your David on! It was David who wrote Psalm 23, which reads:

The LORD is my shepherd; I shall not want. He maketh me to lie down in green pas-

tures: he leadeth me beside the still waters. He restoreth my soul: he leadeth me in the paths of righteousness for his name's sake. Yea, though I walk through the valley of the shadow of death, I will fear no evil: for thou art with me; thy rod and thy staff they comfort me. Thou preparest a table before me in the presence of mine enemies: thou anointest my head with oil; my cup runneth over. Surely goodness and mercy shall follow me all the days of my life: and I will dwell in the house of the LORD for ever.

God is with you! His purpose, His plans, His calling over your life! Whatever you may be facing, remember that if God called you to it, He will bring you through it!

Pray this prayer:

Gracious and heavenly Father, thank you for wonderfully creating me. Thank you for knowing me before forming me in the womb. Thank you for setting me apart before I was born. Thank you for your plans for my life, plans to prosper me and not to harm me, plans to give me hope and an expected end. Forgive me for my sins and shortcomings, forgive me for ever doubting you. Prepare me, Lord, for your purpose. Anoint me like David that I might reach my destiny and fulfill my purpose in you. Search my heart God and cast out anything that is not of you. Fill me with your Spirit, fill me with your fruit. Make me like David, Lord. In Jesus's name, amen.

3

Do You Know Where You're Going To?

I taught this sermon during a month where we were learning about our theme for the month: **CHOICES.** Choices are defined as the right, power, or opportunity to choose; option; to prefer or decide (to do something). **Life is all about choices!** The choices that we make determine the direction of our lives. In and throughout our lives including our past, present, and future, every single day of our lives, we make choices. We make simple choices like yes or no, stop or go, do or don't, and whether we will or won't. That's my Jesse Jackson impersonation. We make choices whether to give up or fight. We make choices whether to do wrong or do what is right. We make choices whether to build up or tear down, whether to speak out or be silent. We choose our attitudes and our responses. We choose our actions and behaviors. Again, life is full of choices. It's important to know that God has given us the freedom to make our own choices. We have free will, and God will not violate this free will and force us to do his will or the right thing. We find biblical evidence of this in book of Joshua 24:15 which reads:

> **And if it seem evil unto you to serve the LORD, choose you this day whom ye will serve; whether the gods which your fathers served that were on the other side of the flood, or the gods of the Amorites, in whose land ye dwell:**

but as for me and my house, we will serve the LORD. (John 24:15 KJV)

In fact, the society we live in today continues to send messages and stress to us our right to choose, such as we are currently experiencing in our laws and legislature for example with same-sex marriage. But Satan along with our society, while they continue to stress that you have a "right to choose," the deception and the reality that is left out is that our choices also have consequences. The most important or severe of these consequences is the reality that ultimately it is our choices, our decisions, that affect the direction of our lives. In this sermon, we take a look into the DNA or creation of man and how are unique creation ties into the choices that we make in life. We will also look at how the choices that we are making in our lives ultimately serve as indicators and even predictors in answering the important question of, "Do you know where you're going to?"

Man was created as a trichotomy or, to explain it in simple terms, as a three-part division. These three parts consist of a body, spirit, and soul. Each of us is a spirit who has a soul, and we live in these earthly bodies. Our soul is also comprised of three parts, which consist of our mind, will, and our emotions. Our emotional patterns tend to form our personalities. The way we react to the information that our minds take in, the things we hear and see, the things that happen to us in life and what we choose to receive as truth causes our soul to become what it is or as the scriptures say, as a man thinketh in his heart so is he (Proverbs 23:7). To break it down and illustrate how the three parts of our soul works, from the Bible, we know that without faith it is impossible to please God. We know that faith comes by hearing and hearing by the Word of God. So for those of us who are saved, and I pray that everyone reading this either is or will be in the name of Jesus, amen, and for those of us who already are, when you heard the gospel and good news of Christ and salvation, your heart and your emotions reacted, and those reactions went to work based on the information you took in your mind, which is your intellect or reasoning. With that, your spirit began to bear witness; and lastly, it was your free will by faith that you made a choice to believe and receive the good news you heard as truth, and by mouth, you made a confession unto salvation. Glory to God!

The Bible teaches that Satan came to steal, kill, and destroy. The Bible says that Satan walks to and fro seeking whom he might devour. One of the ways that Satan succeeds in devouring us is through spiritual warfare. In spiritual warfare, Satan uses accusations, temptation, and deception. He is the great deceiver. He uses these strategies so that as I just explained, we react to the information that our minds take in, the things we see and hear instead of walking by faith and not by sight as the Bible instructs us to do. Satan plants seeds to create strongholds, which are incorrect thinking patterns in our lives. Through this, what the enemy knows and what is important that we know is the importance and power of our choices! Know that Satan has no control or power over you! I know that we've probably all heard somebody say the all familiar line, "The devil made me do it," but I'm sorry, no, he didn't! He may have suggested or even hyped you up to do it, but ultimately, it was you that did it! Yes, you did it! And not only did you do it, but tell the truth and shame the devil, you probably liked it! Satan knew you wanted to do it, so he set you up and sent you off because remember he knows exactly what you like; that's why it's called temptation.

But the enemy has no power over you. The Bible says that greater is he that is in me than he that is in world (1 John 4:4). In Luke 10:19, Jesus said, "I have given you authority over all the power of the enemy." God has given you power! With this power, God has also given us free will! And this free will, which is a part of our soul—again our mind, will, and emotions—this is where and how we exercise our freedom of choices. So we as human beings we have free will. We as Christians we also have freedom. We are free, amen! He who the son has set free is free indeed! Jesus Christ, our Lord and Savior, already paid the price on Calvary, which makes us free. We are no longer slaves to sin. But Satan wants to arrest you! He wants to steal your freedom! And the only way that he can achieve this since he has no power over you is through influencing your choices. So as you read this message, if you don't get anything else from this, know Satan's plan and, most importantly, know the power you have and the importance of your choices.

Let's look at some of the many choices that we make. We choose what we eat, whether it is healthy or not. We choose what we put in our bodies be it vitamins and proteins, drugs and alcohol, or even water or juice. We choose our friends, good or bad. We choose our partners and who we will marry. You chose your baby mama or baby daddy, maybe not wisely or purposely, but hey these are some of the choices that we make. Think about the many mottos, worldly beliefs, and the foolishness we hear from others. People say life is all about getting all that you can. Others believe and say that life is all chance. Others say that life is all about the haves versus the have-nots. I've often heard people say that life is all about money and power. With so many belief systems and with so many different ways to turn, what I want to stress to you today is so vital because life is about none of these things. Life is all about choices! Ultimately, we choose the direction of our lives! As I was preparing this message and studying and reading my Bible, it came to me that this entire Bible is full of history and examples, stories, parables, council, wisdom, advice, both blessings and curses, consequences, repercussions, and warnings about choices. The choices that those before us, along with us, and even those after us will have to make. I mean we can start in the book of Genesis with the story of creation and Adam and Eve, and their choice or decision made to eat of the fruit from the forbidden tree. I could take you through the entire Bible into the book of Revelations where one of the final scriptures of the Bible warns us of the plagues should anyone choose to add anything to what is written or subtract from any of the words from this book of prophecy. The Bible is full of choices.

Allow me to share with you just a few more scriptures as evidence of the importance and power of our choices. In Deuteronomy 30:11–20, Moses is talking to the children of Israel giving them all the laws God had commanded him to pass onto them.

The Choice of Life or Death

**"This command I am giving you today
is not too difficult for you to understand, and**

it is not beyond your reach. It is not kept in heaven, so distant that you must ask, 'Who will go up to heaven and bring it down so we can hear it and obey?' It is not kept beyond the sea, so far away that you must ask, 'Who will cross the sea to bring it to us so we can hear it and obey?' No, the message is very close at hand; it is on your lips and in your heart so that you can obey it. "Now listen! Today I am giving you a choice between life and death, between prosperity and disaster. For I command you this day to love the Lord your God and to keep his commands, decrees, and regulations by walking in his ways.

So Moses is commanding this, but still, it's a choice.

If you do this, you will live and multiply, and the Lord your God will bless you and the land you are about to enter and occupy. "But if your heart turns away and you refuse to listen, and if you are drawn away to serve and worship other gods, then I warn you now that you will certainly be destroyed. You will not live a long, good life in the land you are crossing the Jordan to occupy. "Today I have given you the choice between life and death, between blessings and curses. Now I call on heaven and earth to witness the choice you make. Oh, that you would choose life, so that you and your descendants might live!

You can make this choice by loving the Lord your God, obeying him, and committing yourself firmly to him. This is the key to your life.

Can you see how important your choices are? (Continued scripture.)

And if you love and obey the Lord,

Again, your choice.

you will live long in the land the Lord swore to give your ancestors Abraham, Isaac, and Jacob." (Deuteronomy 30:11–20 NLT)

Life, the Bible, all about choices. If you choose, if you choose to do this, then this will be the result. However, if you choose to do otherwise, then this is what will happen. Can you see it? Here is another example:

Blessed is the man that walketh not in the counsel of the ungodly,

Or who do not follow evil men's advice some versions say.

Nor standeth in the way of sinners,

So those who don't hang around with sinners

nor sitteth in the seat of the scornful. (Psalm 1 KJV)

I want to stop here for just a second to talk about scornful, bitter people. Bitter people will always find the negative in everything, even in the move of God. I can recall back when I was an associate pastor at a church that we were just starting, and we began having service in a community center. Within months, we had moved into a hotel banquet room, and within six months to a year, we were preparing to purchase a building. It was the bitter people that didn't want to move. It was the bitter people that were saying that we were moving too fast and that we couldn't afford it. In my experiences, I have also observed that when you don't listen to the bitter people, or when they don't get their way, bitter people will start rumors and start talking against your plans saying, and I believe even praying that you fail. Scornful, bitter people are dangerous! The psalmist is telling us don't surround yourself with scornful, bitter people! If you are sitting next to a bitter person right now as you are reading this, I encourage you to move and find a quiet place. Otherwise, they may start asking you questions, like what are your reading and why? If you want to know how to tell who the bitter, scornful people are, I'll let you know. I ain't scared! Proverbs 6 says that there are seven things that are an abomination to God and scornful, bitter people hit all seven. They have a proud look, a lying tongue, hands that shed innocent blood, a hear that deviseth wicked imaginations, feet that are swift in running mischief, a false witness that speaketh lies, and he that soweth discord among brethren. Again, I urge you to look around you. Look at the people that are a part of your life. Is there anybody that fits this description? If so, from such individuals, RUN! Let's get back to Psalm 1:

> **Blessed is the man that walketh not in the counsel of the ungodly, nor standeth in the way of sinners, nor sitteth in the seat of the scornful. But his delight is in the law of the LORD; and in his law doth he meditate day and night.**

Choices. If you do the above, then this is what will happen. This is what you can expect.

> **And he shall be like a tree planted by the rivers of water, that bringeth forth his fruit in his season; his leaf also shall not wither; and whatsoever he doeth shall prosper. The ungodly are not so: but are like the chaff which the wind driveth away. Therefore, the ungodly**

shall not stand in the judgment, nor sinners in the congregation of the righteous.

For the LORD knoweth the way of the righteous: but the way of the ungodly shall perish.

We're talking about choices, life, the Bible, all about and full of choices! Let's look to the New Testament and what Jesus said. In the Gospel of Matthew chapter 18, the disciples asked Jesus which of them would be the greatest in the kingdom of heaven. Jesus called a small child over and sat the child among them and told them unless you turn to God from your sins and become as little children (choice), you will never get into the kingdom of heaven. Jesus said therefore anyone who humbles himself as this little child (choice) is the greatest in the kingdom of heaven. He also goes on to give them a warning in Matthew 18:6, where he says, but if any of you causes one of these little ones who trusts in me to stumble or lose his faith, so if you make this choice, Jesus says it would be better for you to have a rock tied to your neck and be thrown into the sea. This is proof that God loves the children as should we!

One last example I will share from the Gospel of Matthew 19. Some may recall the story of the rich young ruler who came to Jesus with the question, "Good Master, what must I do to have eternal life?" Jesus told the man that you can get to heaven if you keep the commandments. "Which ones?" the man asked.

Jesus replied, "Don't kill, don't commit adultery, don't steal, don't lie, honor your father and mother, and love your neighbors as yourself."

"I've always obeyed every one of them," the man replied. "What else must I do?"

At that moment, Jesus gave him a choice. This was a choice that Jesus had given to many others before him. Recall when Jesus saw two brothers Peter and Andrew fishing with a net in a boat. Jesus told them, "Come along with me, and I will show you how to fish for the souls of men." He also saw two other brothers, James and John, sitting in a boat fishing with their father Zebedee and called them to come as well. The Bible says at one they stopped their work and leaving their father behind went with Jesus. So Jesus was giving this young ruler the same choice or option that had been given to others before him. This man standing before Jesus asking what else must he to do be saved, Jesus told him in Matthew 19:21, "If you want to be perfect, go and sell everything you have and give the money to the poor, and you will have treasure in heaven; and come, and follow me." Now unlike Peter and Andrew as well as James and John, who left their father behind to follow Jesus, the Bible says that this man made a different choice. The Bible record that when the young man heard Jesus, he went away sadly, for he was very rich. Wow! He chose his riches over following Jesus! What profit a man to gain the whole world but lose his soul? Choices. I'm showing you how life and how the Bible are both all about choices! I'm showing you how powerful and how important our choices are! I'm showing you how ultimately your choices, the choices that we make, determine our destiny! The choices that we make determine the direction of our lives. Your Bible is full of choices. **BIBLE** (**B**asic **I**nstructions **B**efore **L**eaving **E**arth). It's basic instructions, but you choose whether to follow them or not. Before leaving this earth, we should all know that we will leave this earth. There is no question about that! The Bible says that earth and sky will pass away, the world and all its desires. So that's not even a question. As the old gospel song by The Winans says, the question is, which leads me to the title of this sermon, "**DO YOU KNOW WHERE YOU'RE GOING TO?**

Now that's not an original title or creation of mine. As you become more familiar with me as well as reading my sermons, you will learn that I love music, and I enjoy taking it back to the old school. Those of you that are old school should recognize the title of my sermon as being the theme song from the movie *Mahogany*. The song was sung by Diana Ross who also starred in the movie as a character by the name of Tracy Chapman. The movie also starred Billy D.

Williams, who probably most of you ladies, including my mama, used to be crazy about. He played a character by the name of Brian Walker who was Diana Ross's boyfriend in the movie.

This movie was produced by Motown and Barry Gordy and debuted back in 1975, which is the year that I was born. Some of you reading this who are younger than me may not know anything about this, but basically *Mahogany* was a movie about Tracy, an aspiring designer from the slums of Chicago, who puts herself through fashion school with hopes of becoming one of the world's top designers. In the movie, she meets Brian; and shortly after meeting, they fall in love. She then gets discovered and finds herself on a fast rise to the top. Her ambition leads her to Rome, and she is forced to choose between the man she loves and her dream to become rich and famous, which she thinks will bring happiness. She learns from Brian one of the most memorable quotes from the movie which is that "success is nothing without someone you love to share it with." So that's a brief summary of the movie. I said all of that to get back to the title and theme song for the movie, which is also the title for this sermon. The title is a question that we all need to ask ourselves, do you know where you're going to? The lyrics of the song are the following:

> Do you know where you're going to?
> Do you like the things that life is showing you?
> Where are you going to?
> Do you know?

As we have spent time in this sermon with learning the importance of our choices, and as we begin to apply what we've learned regarding the choices we make in our daily lives, Christian walks, and in determining the direction of our lives and destiny, it is vital not only that we know the answer to what Mrs. Diana Ross sung about, but also that we know how it is that we are going to get there! Another line in the song asks, "Do you get what you're hoping for?"

We always hear about faith. If there is one word that Christians should know, it's faith! What is faith? Hebrews 11:1 says:

Now faith is the substance of things hoped for, the evidence of things not seen. (Hebrews 11:1 KJV)

Hebrews 11:6 teaches us that without faith, it is impossible to please God. The Bible makes it clear that faith is necessary. But in order to answer this next question posed by Mrs. Diana Ross, which again is, do you get what you're hoping for? Along with the sermon title and initial question asked, do you know where you're going to? I'm sorry, but faith alone won't get you there. Now some may choose to argue this, but if you don't believe me, I challenge you to do this. Hop in a cab one day and when the driver asks you, "Where to?" Don't say anything! Just sit there! Or try this even, again when the driver asks you, "Where to?" Answer by just saying, "Home." Let's see if you get there! Now I know my example may sound stupid, but this is the way that many of us live our lives. We know faith or so we think. We can tell others how great our faith is. But faith without works is dead (James 2:26)! You have to do something! Where are your works?

Recall the biblical account of the lady with the issue of blood for twelve years. She had faith. But she also lined her faith up with works. She had been to many doctors. She had spent all she had to no avail. But this woman still didn't give up! This woman heard about Jesus and his miracles, and she believed, she had faith that if only she could touch the hem of him! So she found Jesus, which couldn't have been an easy task as Jesus was always on the move. But she found Jesus, and when she found Jesus the Bible records that she pressed her way through the crowds, because again faith without works is dead! So here we are, many of us coming to church every week, some of us twice a week, asking the church to pray for us. Now that's not the issue. There is nothing wrong with that. But if you're asking the church to pray for you because it's been eleven months that you've been without a job, and you keep saying that you have faith and you're not giving up, but you haven't filled out any applications in over three months. You haven't called to check in with the temp services in three weeks. I'm sorry but stop praying, along with asking others to pray, for God to bless what you're not doing!

In the introduction, we read Psalm 1. Psalm 1 says,

Blessed is the man that walketh not in the counsel of the ungodly, nor standeth in the

way of sinners, nor sitteth in the seat of the scornful. But his delight is in the law of the Lord; and in his law doth he meditate day and night.

Those were his choices! These were his works! And because of this, verse 3 says,

And he shall be like a tree planted by the rivers of water, that bringeth forth his fruit in his season; his leaf also shall not wither; and whatsoever he doeth shall prosper.

You have to do something! You must make a choice to be a doer! It's not good enough; it's not sufficient to be just a hearer of the word. You must be a doer! TD Jakes said this, "I ought to be able to tell what it is that you're praying for by looking at what it is that you're working on!" What this means is in the example I provided before, if you're praying for a job, then we ought to be able to tell that by seeing the applications and résumés you've been updating and filling out relentlessly. We ought to be able to see the countless interviews that you've been going on along with interviewing skills that you've been practicing. To my young people, if you've got dreams and you're praying to become a doctor or lawyer, then we ought to see you studying and working hard to get good grades in high school so you can go on to college and take the necessary courses to put yourself in position to receive your degree and many blessings. Those of you who are praying and trying to get a house, we ought to see you working and saving your money along with cleaning up your credit. Men, if you're looking for a wife, and I say men because women you have no business looking for a man. The Bible says that HE who finds a wife finds a good thing. But, women, if he's looking, then still you ought to fix yourself up. Keep your hair done, get your toes painted, and get out of the house so he can find you!

Our choices in life need to line up with our vision! Our choices need to line up with our destiny! The answer to the questions, do you know where you're going to? Do you like the things that life is showing you? If you don't, then maybe the first and best place that you should look is in the mirror. Look at yourself and look at the choices that you are making. I'm not judging, I'm just keeping it real! But if you're spending the majority of your time drinking and smoking and riding around with your crew, then it's safe to say that you are not on your way to finding a job or college. It's safe to say that you are most likely on your way to jail or even worse death. So do you know where you're going to? If these are the types of choices that we make in our lives, if it is our destiny, if where we are going is dependent upon the choices that we make, then what needs to happen is that we need to be transformed by the renewing of our minds that we might have these instructions **(BIBLE)**, wisdom, God's word in our hearts, that we might make the right choices.

As I said earlier, we have power over Satan. Satan knows this! Satan also knows that we have been given free will, which becomes his window of opportunity. Remember we are a trichotomy, meaning we have a body, spirit, and soul. Our bodies are dying daily! Sin entered the world and because of sin death. But Jesus died for our sins, and because he died, we have been reconciled to God. We are saved through Christ. When Jesus saved us, what he saved was our spirit, not our mind! So our bodies are dying, our spirit is saved, there is one more part to us, our soul, which is also composed of three parts, our emotions, will, and mind. Satan knows this, and so again this is where he tries to attack us. The Bible says that,

> **God is a Spirit: and they that worship**
> **him must worship him in spirit and in truth.**
> **(John 4:24 KJV)**

I'm saved. My spirit is saved. But every day, I struggle with my mind! I don't know about you. You can act like it's just me and like your mind isn't still going through some issues. That's fine if you want to act like that. I'll just keep it one hundred by myself if I have to! But I can tell you that, IT'S MY MIND! EVERY DAY IT'S A STRUG-

GLE GOING ON IN MY MIND! It's my spirit versus my flesh! My spirit indeed is willing, but my flesh is weak!

I know if the apostle Paul were reading this today, he would definitely give me an amen. It was Paul who wrote in Romans chapter 7 saying, "I don't understand myself at all!" Paul said, "I really want to do what is right, but I can't!" Paul said, "I do what I don't want to, what I hate." He said, "I know perfectly well that what I am doing is wrong, and my bad conscience proves that I agree with these laws I am breaking, but I can't help myself." You're not alone, Paul. Me, you, Paul, matter of fact, me, you, Paul, Scarface, Bushwick, and Willy D, also known as the Ghetto Boys, as a song they made back in the day says, "My minds playing tricks on me." Yes, my mind plays tricks on me. And if any of you who are reading this feels like keeping it real, then you too will admit that sometimes your mind does the same! My spirit is saved, but my mind is still going through a transformation. In my mind, I'm still dealing with some issues. Transformation is a process! This means that my mind still gives me options or choices. So if you come up to me talking crazy, my mind begins to give me options on how I should respond to you. Should I yell at you? Should I cuss you out? Back in the day, I may have even knocked you on your back pockets! I'm not the only one! Thank God for deliverance! But our minds still give us options.

The mind isn't saved, and because of this, we face an everyday struggle to cast down and work with our minds that we might be transformed by the renewing of our minds. Only then are we able to make the right choices from the options in our minds. For example, the Bible teaches us to be angry but sin not. So as I explained before, when you come up to me talking crazy, I need to make sure that I have the Word of God in my mind and in my heart. David said, "Thy word have I hid in my heart that I might not sin against thee" (Psalm 119:11). It's an everyday struggle just to regulate our minds! Satan wants to control you mind! Why? Because you will always go where you are thinking! Satan knows this, so as I said earlier, he will attempt to deceive you. Satan will make suggestions; he will tempt you. The enemy will tell you that it's your right to choose such as with what I spoke about earlier with the world that we live in and the laws that are being passed today. But Romans 12 tells us to be not conformed to this world but be ye transformed by the renewing of your mind, that ye may prove what is that good, and acceptable, and perfect will of God (Romans 12:1–3). But true transformation starts on the inside saints. It's not the outside. It's easy to change or fix the outside, and that's the problem! That's what we're doing. Far too many of us are sitting in churches across the nation acting, being actors just as good as Diana Ross and Billy D. Williams in *Mahogany*. We're acting as if we've transformed when in reality, we've done nothing more than put on a longer dress and a crown hat! We've done nothing but pull up our pants and went to the barbershop and got a haircut and went and bought a suit. Transformation is a process that starts on the inside!

We also cannot ignore the first part of Romans 12, which tells us to not be conformed to this world. Conformed means to shape around. Don't shape yourself around this world, around worldly people, don't do what they do. When people come in the church and try to dress up the outside only, we can still tell who you've been with all week. All week they been hanging with negative, scornful, bitter, worldly people. Six days out the week you been with Ray Ray and Pookie, then you come in church on Sunday morning and the praise team, and the pastor is supposed to prime and pump you up! It's no wonder why you can hardly lift your hands and say amen. It's no wonder why you can't stand up and give God some praise. What have you been feeding yourself all week? Because your mind becomes what it eats. You become what you are around. You become what you read and talk all week. What you watch on TV all week. You become who you've been with all week. If you want to truly be transformed, you have to watch what you feed your mind. If you change what you feed your mind, you will change your thinking. Again, this is ever important to remember because you will always go where it is that you are thinking. Satan wants to control your mind! The constant struggle going on in your mind between spirit and flesh, your old nature and your new life. The sin that Paul said was inside him and stronger than him. That flesh man that was at war with his mind and winning the fight thus making him a slave to sin. That flesh man that was causing him to make the wrong choices. You have to kill that old man! The word tells us that he that is in Christ is a new creature! Old things have passed away and behold all things become anew! (2 Corinthians 5:17). Renew your mind! That's why the Bible tells us in Philippians 2:5–8:

> **Let this mind be in you, which was also in Christ Jesus: Who, being in the form of God, thought it not robbery to be equal with God: But made himself of no reputation, and took upon him the form of a servant, and was made in the likeness of men. (Philippians 2:5–8 KJV)**

He was made like us!

> **And being found in fashion as a man, he humbled himself, and became obedient unto death, even the death of the cross.**

Jesus died! He died that we might live! And not only is it his will that we have life but that we have life more abundantly! **YOU SHOULD LIKE THE THINGS THAT LIFE IS SHOWING YOU!**

Now, just because Jesus died that you might live doesn't mean that automatically you have eternal life. As I've always taught, you have a choice! Yes, you have a choice in this matter. Choose ye this day whom you will serve! Just as Jesus Christ made a choice at Calvary to lay down his life and be crucified. Today, I invite you to choose the same!

In Galatians 2:20, one of my favorite scriptures, Paul said,

> **I am crucified with Christ: nevertheless I live; yet not I, but Christ liveth in me: and the life which I now live in the flesh I live by the faith of the Son of God, who loved me, and gave himself for me. (Galatians 2:20 KJV)**

Do you know where you're going to? The choices you make in life will determine where you go in life as well as when you leave this life. As you go higher and higher in life, as you make the right choices and resist the devil and his temptations, his deceptions, as God promotes you to new levels, I want you to understand that it might get lonelier and lonelier. But know that this is because where God is taking you to destiny, to that place he has called you to be, everybody that's with you right now won't be able to go with you. But don't feel bad, don't let that get you down. The Bible tells us that even heaven can be entered only through the straight and narrow gate. But the way that leads to destruction, that highway to hell is broad and its gate wide enough for all the multitudes that choose its easy way. There it is again, choices. But the gateway to life is small, and the road is narrow and only a few ever find it. This is one time where it's okay for you to be narrow-minded! I encourage you not to focus on those that fall off in your life, focus on where God is taking you. Often in our lives when God allows us to lose some things or some people and relationships, he allows it so that we can seek him and learn to depend on him more and more. I am at that point in my life now where I don't care about you not talking to me or not liking me. For I know whom I am in Christ! I know what God has called me to do, and I know where he's taking me! So I don't care if people say that it's lonely at the top! Honestly, I feel like it's too crowded; it's too many haters at the bottom! It's too many bottom-feeders! I'm going to the top! As the old gospel song we used to sing says, "I'm going up yonder!"

They normally sing that song at funerals. So as I close this sermon, I believe that maybe you should have a funeral today. Luke 17:33 says,

Whoever clings to his life shall lose it, and whoever loses his life shall save it. (Luke 17:33 TLB)

This funeral service, which I'm speaking of, starts right now. The choices you've made in your life, some of the choices that you are still making, these choices are either blessing you with life and life more abundantly as Christ purposed for you to have. Or the choices that you are making are killing you, your purpose, and your destiny. Think about the song, sermon title, and question, do you know where you're going to? Do you like the things that life is showing you? Think about the choices and decisions that you make every day and how these choices are impacting where it is that you're going to both positively and negatively. Now for this to be a funeral service, somebody must die! So for this funeral service, I want you to get some paper and what I want you to do is kill your flesh man! This is how we're going to do this. Whatever it is that's hindering you from walking into your destiny, anything that is not helping you to get to where it is that God purposed for you to be, whatever it is whether its anger, pride, addiction, doubt, fear, lust, I want you to write it down and we're going to bring it before God and ask that he kill that flesh man and allow our flesh as Paul spoke of to be crucified with Christ. Write down the things in your life including your strongholds, the behavior, and the choices you've made that are hindering your walk, your destiny, and where it is that you are trying to go in life.

Whatever it is, write it down, and we are going to pray over it today; and after you have prayed over it, I want you to throw it away, burn or bury it, so that it might never rise up again in you! And that today you might know without a shadow of a doubt where it is that you are going to. Write it down and say this prayer:

> **Gracious and heavenly, Father, thank you for this day. Thank you for your forgiveness, grace, and mercy that has kept me to this hour. Thank you for knowing and loving me yet while I was in my mother's womb. Thank you for saving me and sanctifying me. Thank you for your purpose and plans for my life. Lord, I ask for your forgiveness now. Forgive me for my sins and shortcomings both known and unknown. Forgive me for the choices, which I have made contrary to your will. Forgive me**

for every step that I've strayed from your path. Bless me to kill my flesh man. Let me decrease in my flesh that I might increase in your spirit. Search my heart, Lord. Whatever you find that is not of you, any fruit of the flesh that exist, I ask that you remove it Lord and fill me with your Spirit and fruit thereof. These things that I have written down today I bring before you and ask that you will deliver me from these evils that they may never rise in me again. Like Paul, I declare that I have been crucified with Christ nevertheless I live; yet not I, but Christ liveth in me: and the life which I now live in the flesh I live by the faith of the Son of God, who loved me, and gave himself for me. Bless me on this day that I might forever know where it is that I am going to and that I may be overjoyed with the things that life is showing me. In Jesus's name, amen.

4

Connections/Disconnect Your Connections?

Think about any appliance in your home. Your refrigerator, stove, microwave, radio, television, or computer, no matter the brand or cost, they are all useless without power. They must be plugged in or "connected" to the appropriate power source in order to operate effectively and efficiently. This same principle applies to us. Have you ever felt as if you are just not being productive in life? Have you ever felt powerless or as if your life was at a standstill? You may need to check your connections. Who or what are you connected to, and how are these connections impacting your life? This sermon is a reminder that your power is in your connections.

Our scripture for this sermon is found in the book of 2 Corinthians 6:17–18 (KJV). It reads:

> **Wherefore come out from among them, and be ye separate, saith the Lord, and touch not the unclean thing; and I will receive you. And will be a Father unto you, and ye shall be my sons and daughters, saith the Lord Almighty. (2 Corinthians 6:17–18 KJV)**

I want to talk to you about connections, in particular the power in and of your connections. The passage, which you just read, was the second epistle or letter written by the Apostle Paul to the church of God in Corinth or the Corinthians. In this letter, out of love, Paul is trying to encourage the Church of Corinth warning them to stay away from certain things. In this particular passage, the warning is against idolatry. Idolatry, of course, meaning not only the worship of idols, but idolatry is also extreme admiration, love, or reverence for something or someone. If you were to back up just a little in 2 Corinthians 6:14–16 (NIV), you'll see where Paul writes to the church giving this warning against idolatry telling them: "**Do not be yoked.**"

Yoked means joined or coupling.

> **Do not be yoked together with unbelievers. For what do righteousness and wickedness have in common? Or what fellowship can light have with darkness? What harmony is there between Christ and Belial?**

Belial is a Hebrew word, which basically means evil, wickedness, or worthlessness, ungodly.

Verse 15 continued:

> **Or what does a believer have in common with an unbeliever? What agreement is there between the temple of God and idols? For we are the temple of the living God.**

Allow me to point out that this is another place in the Bible where we can see that, "You are the Church."

Verse 16 continued:

> **As God has said: "I will live with them and walk among them, and I will be their God, and they will be my people."**

This leads us back to our sermon scripture where again Paul is instructing the church writing,

Wherefore come out from among them, and be ye separate, saith the Lord.

The word *separate* used in this verse translates from the Greek word *Aphoriza*, which means to set off by boundary. This brings me to my first point, which is that what this means for each of us is that we all ought to have some boundaries! Again, I repeat, you ought to have some boundaries! Those of us professing to be Christians, those of us professing to be born again, to be followers of Jesus Christ, you have to have some boundaries! There should be some things that you don't say as well as some things that you don't do! In your life, some things should be out of bounds! There should be some places that you don't go, at least anymore! The reason for this we find in the Word of God in which it was also the Apostle Paul also writes in 2 Corinthians 5:17:

Therefore if any man be in Christ, he is a new creature: old things are passed away; behold, all things are become new. (2 Corinthians 5:17 KJV)

And lastly, there should also be some people or things that you don't touch or connect with! So Paul is warning the church,

Wherefore come out from among them, and be ye separate, saith the Lord, and touch not the unclean thing; and I will receive you.

I preached a sermon a long while ago where I spoke about the 5P's and disconnecting your connections. The 5P's being a spinoff from the original 7P's, which is a British army adage used by educators and trainers in military or civilian situations which stands for **Proper Planning and Preparation Prevents Piss Poor Performance**.

I did a spin-off of that to create the 5P's, which stands for **Purpose Planning Produces Power and Prosperity**. It was in that sermon that I spoke about our connections and the power or lack thereof, which comes through or as a result of our connections, for example as with partnerships. It is important that you know that there is power in partnerships! Let's put some Word behind that!

Matthew 18:20 reads:

> **For where two or three are gathered together in my name, there am I in the midst of them. (Matthew 18:20 KJV)**

Ecclesiastes 4:9–12 reads:

> **Two are better than one, because they have a good return for their labor: If either of them falls down, one can help the other up. But pity anyone who falls and has no one to help them up. Also, if two lie down together, they will keep warm. But how can one keep warm alone? Though one may be overpowered, two can defend themselves. A cord of three strands is not quickly broken. (Ecclesiastes 4:9–12 NIV)**

Again, there is power in partnerships! This is why every day in business we hear of companies merging or acquiring other companies to make their organizations stronger and more competitive! These partnerships are strategic in setting these companies up to be successful and able to lead in their industry! Another example includes politics such as when you look at presidential elections. In a presidential election, candidates that are running for president in order to make themselves a stronger candidate and appeal to more voters, candidates will associate themselves and partner with the right contributors. They will also choose a vice president as a running mate such as when Barack Obama selected Joe Biden, and they triumphed over John McCain and his selection of Sarah Palin. This is all evidence that there is power in partnerships! There is power in your connections!

In your own life, think about some of the connections you've made throughout the years including friends and family, spouses, fraternities and sororities, again political and professional connections, and even connections such as club or gang affiliations. Many people say that their reason for joining a gang was because it offered a sense of family, brother, or sisterhood. A sense of unity! It all adds up to there is power in connections! Your connections, who or what you are connected to say a lot about who you are! We've all heard the saying, "Birds of a feather flock together!" Well, in our Bibles, the book of Proverbs says it like this:

> **Be with wise men and become wise. Be with evil men and become evil. (Proverbs 13:20 TLB)**

> **A mirror reflects a man's face, but what he is really like is shown by the kind of friends he chooses. (Proverbs 27:19 TLB)**

Who or what you are connected to has a direct impact and effect on your life! We can again credit Paul for providing to us this warning found in:

> **Do not be misled: "Bad company corrupts good character. (1 Corinthians 15:33 NIV)**

In speaking about power and about connections, let's take a closer look into the meaning of power. The word *power* translates from the Greek word *Exousia*. It means the sense of ability or privilege, force, capacity, competency, freedom or mastery, delegated influence, authority, jurisdiction, liberty, power, right, and strength. You are the salt of the earth! In the English dictionary, *power* is defined as the ability to do or act; the capability of doing or accomplishing something. In dealing with the law of physics, power is the rate at which energy is transferred, used or transformed. An example of this is the rate at which a light bulb transforms electrical energy into heat. With this understanding, we know that light is measured in watts and so the more wattage, the more power and the more electrical energy is used. To further break that down, just think about the appliances in your home that I wrote about in the introduction. All of your appliances and electronics from your refrigerator, stove, stereo, and even your favorite lamp, all run off of power! And again, they are all useless and do us no good until or unless you plug it in until you connect it to the power source. As the Glade commercial says, PLUG IT IN, PLUG IT IN!

Well, church it's the same with us! We have to be connected! So who are you connected to? What are you connected to? It's important that we ask this question and take an inventory in our lives because ultimately it is your connections that are influencing your power! The Bible provides us with knowledge and wisdom and teaches us about both power and connections! The Bible teaches us about the importance and results of our connections along with the consequences! We learn from the Bible that one can be both blessed and cursed based on who or what you are connected to! Who or what you are attached to! The entire human race, the fall of man, the sin that we were all born into and inherited was all through our connection! Death through Adam!

Romans 5:12 reads:

> **Therefore, just as sin entered the world through one man, and death through sin, and in this way death came to all people, because all sinned. (Romans 5:12 NIV)**

It was in our connection to Adam, our connection through flesh, that we were cursed! Again, it was death that came through

Adam, but glory, hallelujah it is life that came through Christ! The Word of God explains in the book of Romans:

> **You see, at just the right time, when we were still powerless, Christ died for the ungodly. Very rarely will anyone die for a righteous person, though for a good person someone might possibly dare to die. But God demonstrates his own love for us in this: While we were still sinners, Christ died for us. Since we have now been justified by his blood, how much more shall we be saved from God's wrath through him! For if, while we were God's enemies, we were reconciled to him through the death of his Son, how much more, having been reconciled, shall we be saved through his life! Not only is this so, but we also boast in God through our Lord Jesus Christ, through whom we have now received reconciliation. (Romans 5:6–11 NIV)**

Verses 18–21 read:

> **Consequently, just as one trespass resulted in condemnation for all people, so also one righteous act resulted in justification and life for all people. For as by one man's disobedience many were made sinners, so by the obedience of one shall many be made righteous. The law was brought in so that the trespass might increase. But where sin increased, grace increased all the more, so that, just as sin reigned in death, so also grace might reign through righteousness to bring eternal life through Jesus Christ our Lord.**

Our power is through our connection! If you are saved today, then you received a divine hookup, a divine connection! The beginning of Romans 5:1–2 reads:

Therefore, since we have been justified through faith, we have peace with God through our Lord Jesus Christ, through whom we have gained access by faith into this grace in which we now stand. (Romans 5:1–2 NIV)

In which we now have power! Do you know that you have power? We have power through our connection! If power comes through our connections, through being connected to the power source, well Jesus is the ultimate power source!

Power is also defined as the possession of control or command over others—authority. So every person who reads this needs to know that you have power, power given to you by God. God has given you authority! In Luke 10:19, the Bible says, look I have given you authority over all the power of the enemy! So you have power even over the enemy! Second Timothy 1:7 is another scripture, which tells us that we have power. It reads:

For God hath not given us the spirit of fear; but of power, and of love, and of a sound mind. (2 Timothy 1:7 KJV)

So those of us that are in Christ and filled with the Holy Spirit, we have power. Just say to yourself out loud, "God is my strength and my power!" While Jesus walked the earth, he anointed or gave his disciples power against unclean spirits to cast them out and to heal sickness and disease. Jesus also promised that greater works shall we do! After Jesus was crucified, he appeared to the apostles telling them that they shall receive power after the Holy Ghost has come upon them. A scripture that you may be familiar with is Ephesians 3:20, which reads:

Now unto him that is able to do exceeding abundantly above all that we ask or think,

**according to the power that worketh in us.
(Ephesians 3:20 KJV)**

Again, we are able to see that Jesus is the ultimate source of power, and our power is in out connections! In getting back to our sermon scripture, Paul is warning the church about who or what it is that we connect ourselves to. He's warning the church to separate! Again, he says:

**Wherefore come out from among them,
and be ye separate, saith the Lord, and touch
not the unclean thing; and I will receive you.
(2 Corinthians 6:17 KJV)**

The unclean thing, don't touch it! Stay away from it! Again, you ought to have some boundaries! Why? Because it can affect you! It can impact you! It can impede you! Who or what you are connected to can impact your power! It can impact where you're going, your destiny! It can impact God's plans for your life! His plans to prosper you and not to harm you! His plans to give you hope and an expected end, a future! As an example, I like to refer to the biblical account found in the Gospels of the rich man that came to Jesus asking him, what must I do to have eternal life? Jesus replied to this man, "Keep the commandments. Don't kill, don't commit adultery, don't steal, don't lie."

The rich man replied to Jesus saying, "I've always obeyed every one of them."

Jesus then said, "If you want to be perfect, go and sell everything you have and give the money to the poor and you will have treasure in heaven, and follow me!"

But we know that this man was too attached to his riches and money! The Bible says that no one can serve two masters! For you will hate one and love the other! The Bible says you will be devoted to one and despise the other! You cannot serve God and money! Come out from among them! Touch not the unclean thing!

In reading the book of Leviticus, you will find where God was establishing his laws amongst the children of Israel. In Leviticus, Moses mentions many actions and behaviors that were forbidden by God and would in fact defile a person or make them unclean. For example, in Leviticus chapter 11, there were certain foods that were considered clean and unclean. Touching dead animals would cause one to be considered unclean, and they would then have to go through a cleansing process and still would not be clean for a period of time. Leviticus chapter 12 describes how a woman after childbirth was considered unclean for a period of seven days as well as when she was on her menstrual cycle. Leviticus chapter 13 speaks about skin diseases and how if a person had certain swelling or rashes, they would have to be examined by the priest to see if they would be considered unclean and what cleansing ceremony they would need to go through. Leviticus chapter 17 talks about sexual contact and relationships that defiled or made a person unclean. All these things are examples that defiled a person! We also know that the children of Israel sinned against God by doing a lot of idol worshipping such as in building a golden calf and following many of the pagan traditions even after being warned by Moses and God that when they went into these foreign lands, to not conform, to not do as the pagans did! They were warned not to practice what they practiced! So Paul is doing the same thing with the Church of Corinth in encouraging them to separate themselves, to come out from among them. Why? So that God will receive you!

And, "I will be a Father to you, and you will be my sons and daughters, says the Lord Almighty." (2 Corinthians 6:18 NIV)

Also, in talking about separation, we know the consequences of sin. Sin separates us from God! The wages of sin is death! In relating sin to power, sin takes your power by separating you from God! I preached a sermon titled "Do It for the Vine." The sermon was inspired by the video entertainment network app and craze Vine.

The scripture in which the sermon was written came from John 15:5 which reads:

> **Yes, I am the vine; you are the branches.**
> **Those who remain in me, and I in them, will**
> **produce much fruit. For apart from me you**
> **can do nothing. (John 15:5 NLT)**

Apart from Jesus, you can do nothing! Apart from Jesus, you have no power! It is God that woke you up this morning! It is God that gave you the power, the ability to get out of bed! It was not by your might nor power, but it was through the power of the Holy Spirit!

Philippians 4:13 reads:

> **I can do all things through Christ which**
> **strengtheneth me. (Philippians 4:13 KJV)**

But without him, you are nothing more than a fancy TV or appliance that might look good but just as well could have stayed in the box because you have no power! The power is in/of our connections!

Consider this analogy. Think about a car battery. If you have ever had your battery go bad in your car and you had to get a jump, then you know that when jumping your car battery, your battery has a positive and a negative hookup. If you've ever used a set of jumper cables, then you know that one is black and the other is usually red. So if you are going to jump your car because your battery has died and needs some power, or even if you are giving somebody else a jump, you have to be careful to make sure that you hook the black cable onto the negative outlet. So you have to be careful to connect the negative to the negative! I hope you're getting this! And you also have to make sure that you connect the positive with the positive; otherwise, you ain't getting no power! So check your connections! If your connections ain't right, the most you might get is a spark or two! I swear I hope you're getting this! Let me explain it another way. Have you ever hooked up or connected with somebody because you thought it was gon' just be all that and then some? But after it was all said and done, you realized that it was nothing but a spark! You might get a spark! Or you also might mess around and cause a short in a perfectly good battery. And now you're left with two bad batteries! All because of your connections! Check your connections!

Who are you connected to? Is it your friends, your boys, your girls? Is it your boo? Is it your family? Is it church folks? Is it folks that don't want anything more out of life, folks that are content with where they are? These types of people are the ones that every time you start talking about doing something more with your life, they infect you with their spirits of doubt and fear. These are the naysayers! Who are you connected to? Is it the haters that you connect with? Is it the folks that instead of trying to get their own they would rather just hate on the folks trying to do something! Who are you connected to? Is it the phony folks that are okay with you as long as you need them and they helping you out? They are okay just as long as you don't get to the point where you are doing better than them! Check your connections! You just might find out that you need to disconnect some connections! You might find out that it's time to separate yourself. This warning from Paul that we see to the Corinthians and now to us this is a warning that was seen several times throughout the Word of God. In Numbers 16:21, God told Moses and Aaron:

> **Separate yourselves from this assembly so I can put an end to them at once. (Numbers 16:21 NIV)**

Ezra 10:11 reads:

> **Now honor the LORD, the God of your ancestors, and do his will. Separate yourselves from the peoples around you and from your foreign wives. (Ezra 10:11 NIV)**

Do not be misled, bad company corrupts good character! We should also know that even in this world, you can be found guilty just by association. You can be an accessory to a crime in which you can be both arrested and convicted! Another saying you may have heard before that remains true is that association brings assimilation. Think about this and how it holds true. Isn't it amazing how soon after meeting someone we can find ourselves unconsciously mimicking their behavior or idiosyncrasies? We don't even have to be around them for that long before we start making hand gestures like them, saying their sayings, and even making a facial expression the way they do. We, in essence, absorb and conform to their behavior. This is why Paul also tells us in the book of Romans 12:

And be not conformed to this world: but be ye transformed by the renewing of your mind, that ye may prove what is that good, and acceptable, and perfect, will of God. (Romans 12:2 KJV)

I once preached a sermon where I spoke about being an overcomer. In the sermon, I spoke about how you can say that you're something or somebody all you want but remember you're still going to have to prove it! You are going to have to pass some tests! You are going to have to actually be an overcomer! So again, our connections, who or what we surround ourselves with, who or what we attach ourselves to remains critical because we all have energy that we transmit to others. Spirits can be transferable! This explains how we can be around someone that is always negative, depressed, or complaining, and we begin to feel down ourselves. Likewise, we can come into the presence of someone who is full of faith, optimism, and upbeat, and we can walk away from a person like that feeling uplifted. We must choose our company wisely. Now I'm not saying that we should stay away from everybody and start labeling folks as sinners doomed to hell. No, we are the light! We are supposed to let our light so shine before men! We are supposed to show others the love of God! But I am talking about those friends and associates that we walk with on a daily basis. I am talking about our religion, those things that we do on a regular or routine basis. I am talking about the places that we go and who we associate with as well as what we associate with. This even includes what we listen to and watch on television daily. We need to watch what we feed our spirit! Checking your connections includes everything you connect to! **Proverbs 4:23** reads:

> **Keep thy heart with all diligence; for out of it are the issues of life. (Proverbs 4:23 KJV)**

Again, we need boundaries! We need separation because again we are not of this world! For God says, I have chosen you out of the world!

Jeremiah 1:5 reads:

> **Before I formed thee in the belly I knew thee; and before thou camest forth out of the womb I sanctified thee, and I ordained thee a prophet unto the nations. (Jeremiah 1:5 KJV)**

The word *sanctified* means set apart, clean, consecrated, to be holy. So we are in this world but not of this world! It is important to always remember this so that you do not become worldly or attached to the things of this world. This is discussed in the book of 1 John 2.

First John 2:15–17 reads:

> **Love not the world, neither the things that are in the world. If any man love the world, the love of the Father is not in him. For all that is in the world, the lust of the flesh, and the lust of the eyes, and the pride of life, is not of the Father, but is of the world. And the world passeth away, and the lust thereof: but he that doeth the will of God abideth for ever. (1 John 2:15–17 KJV)**

So in conclusion, in looking at our connections though we may not think about this often, but many issues that either have occurred or may occur in our lives are due to our environment and surroundings. The people and things that have caused us to lose power or lose our connection! Those appliances I mentioned along with the other things in our homes, which we seldom think about, what's powering these things until we actually lose power. That's when we have to figure out what happened. That's when we ask and seek the answer as to why did it lose power? Sometimes you may find that you blew a fuse, and you have to do a reset. Another reason could be that you were disconnected for one of several reasons such as nonpayment. There could also be times when you might be experiencing an outage in the area in which you live, possibly caused by a storm passing through and during the storm you lost your power! I'm preaching! And so, you have to do some troubleshooting to try and figure out what caused you to lose your power! Right there I can hear the Apostle Paul saying to the Galatians:

You were running a good race. Who cut in on you to keep you from obeying the truth? That kind of persuasion does not come from the one who calls you. (Galatians 5:7–8 NIV)

I remember having to call my cable provider about some problems I was having with my receiver. When you call in about your TV, phone, or internet, when they begin troubleshooting, they start by asking you some questions. They may ask questions such as, "When did this first occur" or "When did you first notice that you no longer had power?" They might also ask, "How long has this been happening?" and "What steps have you taken so far to try and resolve the issue yourself?" This is exactly what we must do in our lives! This is how you check your connections! Who or what it is that you're connected to! You may find as the Apostle Paul is saying today that you need to separate yourself! Come out from among them! Check your connections! Disconnect those connections that are impacting your power!

Hebrews 12:1 reads:

Let us lay aside every weight, and the sin which doth so easily beset *us*, and let us run

with patience the race that is set before us. (Hebrews 12:1 KJV)

Disconnect your connections!

Wherefore come out from among them, and be ye separate, saith the Lord, and touch not the unclean thing; and I will receive you. And will be a Father unto you, and ye shall be my sons and daughters, saith the Lord Almighty. (2 Corinthians 6:17–18 KJV)

Disconnect your connections! This is exactly what God is going to do! Separate the wheat from the chaff!
Matthew 13:49 reads:

This is how it will be at the end of the age. The angels will come and separate the wicked from the righteous. (Matthew 13:49 NIV)

Matthew 25:32 reads:

All the nations will be gathered before him, and he will separate the people one from another as a shepherd separates the sheep from the goats. (Matthew 25:32 NIV)

Today, Jesus is saying connect to me, the ultimate power source! Say this prayer:

Father God, I give you all praise, honor, and glory! I thank you for your grace and mercy as well as for the power in which you have given to me up to and even on this day. You are an omnipotent God! You have all power! Lord, I pray that your will would be done in my life.

I pray that your plans for my life will come to pass. I ask your forgiveness, Lord, for anything or person that I have attached myself to outside of your will. I ask for forgiveness for anything which I have allowed to steal your anointing. I ask that you bless me with the right connections. Bless me with discernment to check my connections. Let no weapon formed against me prosper. Let nothing hinder my walk and connection to you. Anoint me, Lord! Anoint me to do your works, to fulfill your purpose for my life. I declare that I can do all things through Christ which strengthens me. Give me power and authority as you have declared in your word to tread on snakes and scorpions and over all the power of the enemy. Give me power sufficient to the test that I might glorify you, that I might be a blessing unto others. To you all give all praise, honor. and glory, in Jesus's name, amen.

5

Waiting on the Lord (Part 1)

This sermon is titled and addresses one of life's greatest dilemmas, "Waiting on the Lord." Throughout my life, this is an issue, which I have both encountered and contemplated on several occasions. I've often asked myself and God, "What's taking so long?" It is during these critical moments of waiting in life that we have all grown impatient and made the unfortunate mistake of taking matters into our own hands only to make matters worse. Throughout my life, I have grown in wisdom and discovered that many times it was not that I was waiting on God but rather that it was really God who was waiting on me. How do we know if God heard our prayers? How do we know when to stay or when to move? How do we wait on the Lord? I pray this sermon leads you to your answers.

Let me start by asking this question, who likes to wait? My guess is that your answer was "Not me!" Not only in today's society, but I would guess that for all of eternity as part of our human nature, we have never liked to wait! We don't like waiting for anything! And yet, the irony of our lives is that we will spend most or, I'll even go as far as to say, all of our lives waiting! Just think about it, when we were children, we were waiting, and I can recall so many times saying how I just couldn't wait until I was "grown" so that I could do whatever I wanted to. If you were like me, I can also recall as I grew up and went through adolescence I couldn't wait until I turned sixteen so that I could get my driver's license, which for me was a sign and first major feeling of independence. Again, we are always waiting. I'm sure none of us likes to, but we wait at the doctor's office for our name or number to be called. When you go out to eat at a restaurant, you wait to be seated. When you order from a fast-food restaurant, you wait in line whether you go inside or through the drive-through. We wait at red lights. We wait in traffic. We wait for seasons to change, and not just seasons as related to winter, summer, spring, and fall but also the seasons in our lives. We wait on others, and ultimately at some point in our lives, we have all felt or feel as if we are waiting on God. Everyone reading this right now I am sure that you are waiting on something!

Somebody reading this is waiting to hear some news, whether good or bad. Somebody else reading this is waiting to hear back from an application they filled out for employment and you're hoping and waiting for a job interview or the news of employment. Someone else is awaiting some test results. Someone is waiting to graduate from high school or college. Someone reading this now is waiting on Mr. or Mrs. Right. Someone is waiting to get married. On the contrary, someone else reading this is waiting on Mr. or Mrs. Wrong to get out and move on because you just want to be alone. You can't wait to be free! Someone is waiting for a promotion or raise at work. Someone is waiting for a check to come in the mail. Somebody else is waiting on their last payment toward some debt. I know for sure that I have a few friends out there waiting for their last child support payment! Somebody is waiting to move or to buy a home. Somebody is waiting until they can afford to buy a car or a newer car. Life is full of waiting and so in life we have to wait!

With that said, it is important that you come into the realization of knowing that waiting is a part of God's plan! Waiting is both purposed and a part of God's divine design! Evidence of this is found in the book of Isaiah 40:31 which reads:

> **But they that wait upon the LORD shall renew their strength; they shall mount up with wings as eagles; they shall run, and not be weary; and they shall walk, and not faint. (Isaiah 40:31 KJV)**

But in looking at our human nature, naturally, waiting goes against our sinful nature. It contradicts our flesh which is never satisfied and wants everything now and so because of this naturally we don't like to wait. It is in this constant struggle between flesh and spirit that waiting becomes critical to both our condition and lives. With that said the question that we must answer, the issue which we must resolve becomes how should we wait? As waiting becomes everything!

When we look to the Word of God and our Basic Instructions Before Leaving Earth (BIBLE), many of the sins and shortcomings that we see in the Bible are failures related to waiting. For example, recall the story of Moses and the people of Israel in the book of Exodus. When Moses had gone to the top of Mount Sinai to get the tablets from God, the people of Israel got tired of waiting on Moses to come down and demanded that Aaron make them a God to go before them. Aaron then made them a golden calf and built an altar in which the people worshipped and sacrificed unto which only brought God's wrath against them. How many times have you done this? How many times have you gotten tired of waiting, tired of praying to God and decided to take matters into your own hands? And how many times have your plans backfired and only brought more issues or God's wrath upon you. As the Word of God says in the book of Proverbs 19:21:

> **Many are the plans in a person's heart,**
> **but it is the LORD's purpose that prevails.**
> **(Proverbs 19:21 NIV)**

God has a plan for our lives, all of us! For everyone reading this, know that God created you for a purpose! Being that he created you means that he knows you, and he knows his plans for your life! Jeremiah 29:11 reads:

> **For I know the plans I have for you,"**
> **declares the LORD, "plans to prosper you and**
> **not to harm you, plans to give you hope and a**
> **future. (Jeremiah 29:11 NIV)**

The King James version says:

For I know the thoughts that I think toward you, saith the LORD, thoughts of peace, and not of evil, to give you an expected end. (Jeremiah 29:11 KJV)

Again, he knows who you are! Not only does he know who you are, but he knows and sees into your future. God doesn't only know who you are today, but God also knows who you will become! He sees you as a finished product even though today we are all merely works in progress! You also need to know that just as God knows everything about us and knows our future, Satan also knows who we are! Even when we don't know or realize who we are in Christ and the power that we have working within us, Satan knows! And it becomes Satan's mission to stop us from every reaching our full potential and destiny in Christ! It's through our trials and tribulations, it's in waiting that we develop and mature and grow into God's vision of us. And so, it becomes the enemy's goal to stop God's plans for our lives.

But they that wait upon the LORD shall renew their strength; they shall mount up with wings as eagles; they shall run, and not be weary; and they shall walk, and not faint. (Isaiah 40:31 KJV)

In the same way that you cannot give meat or solid food to a baby without harming them, God is not able to fulfill his purpose in us all at once. It takes time. It takes patience. It takes growth. It takes going through numerous tests, trials, and tribulations. And we ought to be thankful that God doesn't give us everything we ask when we ask for it! We ought to be thankful simply because some of the things we asked for would have killed us! Some of our prayers would have led to our ruin!

But it's in the times of waiting, it's during the waiting periods in our lives that Satan goes to work. It's during these periods and times of waiting that we like the children of Israel or even like Abraham's wife, Sarah, we become weary. We start to question and doubt God. We get anxious and worried. We become fearful. We begin to believe Satan's report. We begin to listen to his suggestions.: "You're really in some trouble now!" "You've already messed up, you might as well go all the way!" "You better do whatever you need to do because ain't nobody else gon' help you!" "This is the only way that you are going to make it!"

This is how the enemy sounds. This is what he tells us: "You don't have to go through all of that, there's a much faster way." "Nobody's going to find out!" "Your marriage is over, they don't love you, they don't appreciate you, why should you be faithful to them?" "The reason that you're going through all of this is because you should have done it this way!" "God is not concerned about you. God doesn't care about that. He's not listening to you. He's not going to help you."

This is how Satan plants his seeds and attempts or seeks to steal your blessings. This is how Satan steals your deliverance. This is how Satan carries out his plans to steal, kill, and destroy! He wants to destroy God's plans for your life! He wants to take you off God's path. Again, he knows who you are, and he knows what God has waiting for you if only you can WAIT!

> **But they that wait upon the LORD shall renew their strength; they shall mount up with wings as eagles; they shall run, and not be weary; and they shall walk, and not faint. (Isaiah 40:31 KJV)**

This is exactly what Satan attempted to do to Jesus when Jesus was led by the Spirit into the wilderness to be tempted by Satan. Jesus was fasting; he hadn't eaten anything in forty days and forty nights! Just imagine how weak he had to feel! Just think about whenever you've fasted whether spiritually or maybe even just for a lab test you had to take which required fasting. Just think about having nothing to eat for one day or even half a day for some folks! Jesus was hungry and his flesh had to be weak. But Jesus was on God's plan. He was doing the will of the Father when here comes the enemy trying to catch Jesus while he was weak. That's what the enemy does! He doesn't fight fair! He kicks you when you're down! So here you have Jesus hungry, hadn't eaten in forty days and forty nights, and Satan knows this! Satan also knows who Jesus is, and so he attempts to tempt Jesus. He comes with his temptation, his suggestions, telling Jesus, "If you're really the Son of God, turn these stones into loaves of bread." What else does he do? He also takes Jesus to the peak of a mountain and shows him the nations of the world and all their glory, and he tells Jesus, "I'll give it all to you if you will only kneel and worship me!" Look at how the enemy works. He's a liar, the great deceiver, offering to Jesus what was already his!

This is the same way that the enemy does to you and me! He knows you, he knows your condition. He knows what you desire! He knows what you need! Don't be fooled, Satan knows your poison! He knows your weaknesses. He knows exactly what you like! That's why it's called temptation! If you didn't need it, if you didn't like it, if it wasn't your cup of tea, then it wouldn't tempt you! But he knows! And with his knowledge, his plan is to send you off! His plan is to get you off the path that God has planned for you. To get you off the path of righteousness. He wants you to interfere with God's plans for your life. He wants you to take matters into your own hands. He wants you to blow it, to mess it all up! He wants to take you out of receiving position! He wants to separate you from God. He wants you to fall to sin. He knows, and we need to remember that sin separates us from God. The ultimate struggle with sin and temptation is that sin is actually going about a legitimate need in an illegitimate way! I'll repeat that again because you need to understand this; sin is going about a legitimate need in an illegitimate way. The things that we are seeking, the things that we need, the things that we desire, the things that we are waiting for are legitimate! For example, you need money! There is a joke, which is actually true, that me and my friends say which is that it costs to go outside! Think about it, when you go outside, you have to get in your car and use gas, which both cost money. Wherever it is that you're going to is most likely also going to cost more money. So we legitimately need money! But some of the things that people do to get money are illegitimate. Another example, love, companionship, these again are legitimate needs. However, some of the ways we go about seeking companionship are illegitimate.

But when we get weary, when we get tired of waiting, when we grow full of doubt this is when we get anxious, and we fall. This is why the Word of God tells us in Philippians 4:6

> **Do not be anxious about anything, but in every situation, by prayer and petition with thanksgiving, present your requests to God. And the peace of God, which transcends all understanding, will guard your hearts and your minds in Christ Jesus. (Philippians 4:6–7 NIV)**

I love the Living Bible translation, which says it like this:

> **Don't worry about anything; instead, pray about everything; tell God your needs, and don't forget to thank him for his answers. If you do this, you will experience God's peace, which is far more wonderful than the human mind can understand. His peace will keep your thoughts and your hearts quiet and at rest as you trust in Christ Jesus. (Philippians 4:6–7 TLB)**

God's peace, your thoughts, and your heart quiet and at rest, those are some good things. Would you agree? But when we get anxious, and we don't trust and doubt God, when we don't wait on the Lord and decide to handle things ourselves, we often find that we end up with just the opposite. We end up with no peace. We end up with trouble. You can't rest because when you're out there doing wrong, it's hard to find rest! Believe me, I know sometimes it gets hard! I know sometimes it looks dark and dismal. Throughout this sermon, I've repeatedly shared our sermon scripture from Isaiah 40:31. In the same chapter, verse 30 says:

> **Even the youths shall faint and be weary, and the young men shall utterly fall. (Isaiah 40:30 KJV)**

This is exactly what we are seeing today with our youth. Our youth have legitimate needs, but Satan is sending our youth off and leading them to destruction. Our youth are out here robbing the elderly, restaurants, and gas stations for a few dollars. Our youth are in the streets joining gangs, hustling, selling dope, and losing their lives! Trust me, I know what I'm talking about! I was once one of these youths. I was away in college, studying to become an engineer, possibly on my way to making some good money once I earned my degree. But that was three to four years away, and I saw my guys back home, hustling and making money now! Satan suggested to me that I didn't need to wait three or four years. The devil is a lie!

> **But they that wait upon the LORD shall renew their strength; they shall mount up with wings as eagles; they shall run, and not be weary; and they shall walk, and not faint. (Isaiah 40:31 KJV)**

You gotta wait! Wait on the Lord! Be patient!

> **Be joyful in hope, patient in affliction, faithful in prayer. (Romans 12:12 NIV)**

Romans 8:24 says:

> **For we are saved by hope: but hope that is seen is not hope: for what a man seeth, why doth he yet hope for? (Romans 8:24 KJV)**

You don't have to hope for what you already have. But if you hope for what is not seen, what you don't have yet, then it teaches you to wait patiently and confidently. So though it might be hard, wait on the Lord! And think about it this way, how long did God wait for you? Maybe he's still waiting for you! How patient has God been with you? Somebody reading this say out loud, "I will wait on you, Lord!"

Now that we've established that we will wait on the Lord, let me provide you with some wisdom to help you wait. Satan is always busy, and so even when we've made up in our hearts and minds that we will wait on the Lord, Satan has deceived many into thinking that they are waiting on God when God might really be waiting on you! Remember this: **Waiting on God is not a resignation from all activity, it is submission to God's will.**

So what does it mean to wait? Before we look at the definition of wait, the first thing we need to know about the word *wait* is that the word *wait* is a verb! Now I know for some of us it's been a long time since you may have sat in a classroom, so let me remind you that a verb is an action word! So waiting is an action, again it doesn't mean to do nothing!

Definition of *wait*:

> **1: to stay in place in expectation of:**
> **2: to remain stationary in readiness or expectation (stationary meaning, having a fixed position, not movable)**

As David said in the book of Psalms, and we used to sing in church, "I Shall Not Be Moved"!

> **Therefore, my beloved brethren, be ye steadfast, unmoveable, always abounding in the work of the Lord, forasmuch as ye know that your labour is not in vain in the Lord. (1 Corinthians 15:58 KJV)**

Another definition of *wait* is: **Remaining in the same condition or state, not changing. To be available or in readiness:**

Whatever it is that you're waiting for, whatever it is that you're waiting on, are you ready for it? Are you available? You have to position yourself to be ready! Bishop TD Jakes said this, "I ought to be able to tell what you're waiting on by what you're working on!" This means that if you're asking God to increase you, have you made room in your life? This means that if it's a mate that you're seeking, are you available? Are you ready? Do you know how to be a good husband or wife? So often, we see people in relationships wasting time with people that they know they have no future with. People which they know that God hasn't put in their life! Why? Because they feel as if nothing better has come along. Well guess what, it won't! That man or woman that you been praying for, that you say you been waiting on for so long, they can't find you because you're too busy going back and forth fighting with Ray Ray or Rashida! You're blocking your blessing! You haven't made room in your life! You haven't made yourself available! You're not ready!

That financial blessing you've been praying for. How well have you done with whatever it is that you already have? Have you been faithful? Have you been obedient to the Word of God? Have you been paying your tithes? See, this is the stuff that we don't like to hear. We want folks to lie to us and tell us that our blessing is on the way. We've gotten used to hearing stuff like turn around three times and praise God, and he's going to do something supernatural in your life. Well, the devil is a lie! You can turn around all you want, but until you turn your behavior and your life around, all you gon' get is dizzy! That job you've been praying for, have you stayed committed and dedicated to your search? The Word of God says seek and ye shall find! Have you prepared for what you're asking God for? Have you finished your training or education? Have you updated your résumé? Have you worked on your interviewing skills? That house that you've been praying for, are you working? If you are working, have you been saving your money and budgeting your finances? Are you cleaning up your credit and paying off your debt? Waiting is an action! To wait also means to look forward expectantly. To wait also means to attend as a servant. I remember one of the prayer warrior's brother Shaw. When brother Shaw would pray, he would often say, "Teach me to wait like a waiter." At first, I didn't get it, and I used to say to myself, "What is this old man talking about? What does he mean?" But I thought about it and soon figured it out. Think about when you go out to a restaurant to eat. Normally, a host or hostess seats you at your table. The next person you see after you are seated at your table is normally your waiter or waitress. Now your waiter or waitress, their job is not to sit down with you and do nothing, no, their job is to wait on you! And how is it that they wait on you? They serve you! They take your order, get your drinks, bring your food, and get your refills. In all of this, they serve you! What brother Shaw was saying is that this is the same way that it ought to be with us. As we wait for God, we ought to be working, we ought to be serving! Serving God as well as serving others! What you make happen for others God will make happen for you! This means that if you want a financial blessing, then plant a seed! This means that if you want healing, then pray for the healing of others! You reap what you sow! In Ecclesiastes 9:10, the word reads:

> **Whatsoever thy hand findeth to do, do it with thy might; for there is no work, nor device, nor knowledge, nor wisdom, in the grave, whither thou goest. (Ecclesiastes 9:10 KJV)**

In the Gospel of John 9:4, Jesus says:

> **I must work the works of him that sent me, while it is day: the night cometh, when no man can work. (John 9:4 KJV)**

Jesus also says, "Greater works shall you do!" So within these scriptures, we are able to see that in waiting we must work! Again, you must work! Waiting does not mean doing nothing! The Bible says that if you don't work, you don't eat. Mike Jones added that "if you don't grind, you don't shine, no ifs, ands, or buts, bottom line!" Who? MIKE JONES! Anybody over sixty or under thirty never mind that quote! That's from my upbringing.

Waiting means working, serving. You have to be doing something. Oftentimes, people say and feel as if they are waiting on God to do something in their lives, but as I said before, many times, God has already given you everything that you need to succeed! The Bible says that he who is faithful with little, or few things, can be trusted or is faithful in much. In Matthew 25:29, Jesus says:

> **For the man who uses well what he is given shall be given more, and he shall have abundance. But from the man who is unfaithful, even what little responsibility he has shall be taken from him. (Matthew 25:29 TLB)**

To each of us, God has given something! Everyone reading this you have some gift, some talent, something that God can use to bless you! Work your gift! Work your plan! Work well with whatever it is that you have! God can take what little you have and even what little you do and bless it to become great, abundant! The same God that took five loaves of bread and two fish, which was not enough, it was little. But after God blessed it, it was more than enough to feed over five thousand with leftovers! Or what about the widow who went to Elisha? Her husband had just passed, and he had debt in which the collectors were threatening to take her two sons as slaves to satisfy the debt. She went to Elisha saying that she had nothing. No food, nothing except for a jar of olive oil. Elisha told her to borrow as many pots and pans as she could from friends and neighbors and to go into her house with her sons and pour the olive oil from her jar into the pots and pans. She was obedient doing just what the prophet had instructed, and God blessed her one jar of olive oil so that as she began to pour, it flowed until she had filled every pot, pan, and jar she had in her household and then it stopped! She was then able to sell the oil and pay off her husband's debt and still have enough money left to live on! God is awesome! He can take whatever you have, whatever you do, and use it to bless you! Psalm 1:3 reads:

> **And he shall be like a tree planted by the rivers of water, that bringeth forth his fruit in his season; his leaf also shall not wither; and whatsoever he doeth shall prosper. (Psalm 1:3 KJV)**

The key is this: God can't bless what you have not done! You have to do something! Every day that the Good Lord allows you to see is a blessing, another opportunity to serve, to glorify him! He blesses us to wake up with the activity of our limbs, a sound mind, strength, gifts, and purpose. He has plans for you! He expects something from you! He expects more of you!

> **"For I know the plans I have for you," declares the LORD, "plans to prosper you and not to harm you, plans to give you hope and a future." (Jeremiah 29:11 NIV)**

As I close out part one of this sermon, let me conclude by saying that maybe some of us who believe that we've been waiting on God need to ask ourselves this question today. Are you waiting on the Lord, or is the Lord truly waiting for you?

Say this prayer:

> *Gracious and Heavenly Father, thank you for this day, which you have made and allowed me to see. Thank you for each and every blessing, which you have so graciously bestowed upon me. Thank you for my health and strength. Thank you for a sound mind and the activities of my limbs. Thank you for every gift and thank you for your grace and mercy. Father God, I ask that you forgive me for any-*

time and everything that I have ever taken for granted. Forgive me for any time I may have doubted or questioned you. Lord, forgive me for any time that I have been stagnant, not fruitful, and believing that it was because I was waiting on you. Lord, I believe in your plans for my life. Above all, it is my desire to glorify you by walking in your path and fulfilling your purpose for my life. Lord, help me to see your plan. Reveal to me your will and allow me to know if and when I should be still and waiting on you versus if you are waiting for me. For those situations that I must wait on you, Lord, I ask, Lord, that you teach me to wait like a waiter that I might find favor with and glorify you. Let your will be done in my life, let your blessings come to pass. These prayers I ask in Jesus's name, amen.

6

Waiting on the Lord (Part 2)

In part 1 of this sermon, we addressed one of life's greatest dilemmas, "Waiting on the Lord." We learned that many times in life we may think that we are waiting on God, when God is waiting on us! There are however times in life when we will have to wait on God and his timing. In part 2 of this sermon, we will discuss these instances along with the importance of how we should wait on God. Enjoy!

Let's begin with a short review and recap of what we learned in the first part of this series titled "WAITING ON THE LORD." In part 1, we talked about how our lives are full of waiting. How every day we are always waiting whether it's in our daily commutes with traffic or in our routine responsibilities such as a doctor's appointment. Think back to even when we were kids how much we were waiting. We couldn't wait until we were grown. We couldn't wait until we turned sixteen and got our driver's license. How we wait for seasons to change in our lives, and ultimately, how we wait on God. We learned that in life, we have to wait, and even though we don't like to wait, how critical waiting is to our lives because it is during the waiting periods of our lives that we have experienced most of our setbacks or failures. It is during the waiting periods of our lives that we experience and go through all sorts of emotions, and how we react and respond during these periods based off our emotions, which causes us to take matters into our own hands. This often leads us off God's path and plans for our lives.

In part 1, I told you that waiting was purposed and part of God's divine design. We talked about how God has not forgotten about you and how he has a plan for each of our lives. We also learned how God knows who we are, and not only does he know who we are, but how God is able to see into our future. God knows who we will and have yet become. I gave you scripture from Jeremiah 29:11 which reads"

**"For I know the plans I have for you,"
declares the LORD, "plans to prosper you and
not to harm you, plans to give you hope and a
future. (Jeremiah 29:11 NIV)**

Or **"an expected end"** as the King James Version reads.

I also stated that just as God knows who we are, the enemy, Satan also knows who we are, even when we sometimes ourselves don't realize who we are and the power we have working deep within. Satan knows the strength we have in and through Christ Jesus. Because of this, it becomes Satan's mission to stop God's plans for our lives and to stop us from ever reaching our destiny, fruition, and full potential in Christ. I wrote how just as we are not able to give solid food or meat to an infant without harming them, God is not able to fulfill his purpose in us all at once. It takes time! It is in and through waiting that we develop and mature. It is through the struggles, failures, trials, and tribulations that we grow into God's vision of us. And so again it becomes the enemy's goal to stop God's plans for our lives! I explained that it is in these times and periods of waiting that Satan goes to work. It's during these waiting periods that we become weary and begin to doubt, grow anxious, and become worried. We become fearful, and we begin to believe Satan's report. We begin to listen to his suggestions. Satan plants his seeds, and he seeks and attempts to steal your deliverance and blessings. Ultimately, this is Satan's plan to kill and destroy you. He wants to destroy God's plan for your life. It's worth saying again that Satan knows who you are, and he knows what God has waiting for you if only you could wait!

Do not be anxious about anything, but in every situation, by prayer and petition, with thanksgiving, present your requests to God. And the peace of God, which transcends all understanding, will guard your hearts and your minds in Christ Jesus. (Philippians 4:6–7 NIV)

I told you that it was important that we know that waiting on God does not mean doing nothing! Waiting is not a resignation from all activity. Waiting is submission to God's will. Waiting is a verb, an action word! I gave you some definitions of **wait**:

1. **To stay in place in expectation of.**
2. **To remain stationary in readiness or expectation. Remaining in the same condition or state, not changing.**
3. **To be available or in readiness.**

In part 1, I said that I ought to be able to tell what you are waiting on by looking at what you are working on! Other definitions of waiting include:

4. **To look forward expectantly.**

Which means to have hope or faith.

5. **To attend as a servant.**

Or as Brother Shaw would say, "To wait like a waiter!" So in waiting, we ought to be serving both God and others! I also gave you Psalm 1:3 which reads:

And he shall be like a tree planted by the rivers of water, that bringeth forth his fruit in his season; his leaf also shall not wither; and

whatsoever he doeth shall prosper. (Psalm 1:3 KJV)

God can take whatever you have or whatever you do and use it to bless you! But vice versa, God cannot bless what you have not done! You have to do something! Every day that the Lord allows you to see is a blessing, another opportunity to serve and glorify him! Every morning, God blesses us to wake up with countless blessing such as a sound mind, the activity of our limbs, strength, gifts, and purpose. God has plans for you! He expects something from you! He expects more and more of you! Lastly in part 1, we discussed that even once we've made up in our hearts and minds that we will wait on the Lord, we then need wisdom in order to be sure that we are not being deceived by the enemy into thinking that we are waiting on God when in actuality God just might be waiting on you!

In beginning with part 2 of my sermon, I want to continue our discussion by taking a deeper look into waiting on the Lord. We will do this by focusing on answering the question: how should we wait for the Lord, and specifically, what is it that we should be doing while we are yet waiting? Once you have made up your mind and chosen that you will wait on the Lord and submit to his will and timing, you then need to make the critical decision of choosing how you will wait. How will you wait? As you think about this question, you will begin to realize the severity of how important and critical of a question and decision this is based on the vastness and the many different ways that one can choose to wait. Again, how will you wait? Will you wait well? Will you wait in worry? Will you wait in wonder as in doubt? Will you wait and whine? These are just a few examples of the many different ways that we wait. When we look to our Bibles, we find several recorded examples in which we can gain knowledge and wisdom into waiting.

For instance, we can look to David as an example of one who waited well. As we've discussed, when you look at certain people and watch how they wait and what they do while they wait, you will see certain people that the enemy has deceived. These people are easy to recognize and identify as ones who have been deceived because when you watch them, you will see that they are doing absolutely nothing! Many of you have heard the short story of the drowning or stranded man at sea, but in case you haven't, allow me to share it with you.

There was once a man whose boat had capsized, and he found himself in the unfortunate position of trying to stay afloat while being stranded at sea. Being a God-fearing man and with no help in sight, the man decided to pray to God hoping that the Lord would hear is prayer and save him from this predicament. Shortly after praying, a speedboat passed by and noticed the man struggling to stay afloat and so naturally they circled back and offered to help. The man replied to the passengers in the speedboat, "No, thank you. I'm waiting on the Lord. My God will save me." Not long after a large ocean liner sailed by and the captain of the ship noticed the man struggling to stay afloat and ordered some of his men to lower one of the rescue boats and go save the man. Once the men from the ship reached the now-almost-drowning man, again he replied, "No, thanks. I am certain that my God will save me. I'm waiting on the Lord!" A few hours later, a helicopter flew by and again noticed the man drowning and again attempted to rescue the man by lowering a rope ladder for the man to climb to safety. Again, the man refused and so the helicopter flew away. Shortly after the helicopter left, the man drowned. After the man died, he appeared before God and the first thing the man did was question God saying, "Lord, I trusted and prayed to you. Why didn't you rescue me?" God replied to the man saying, "I sent you a speedboat, an ocean liner, and a helicopter. What more did you expect?"

Now of course when you read this story, it sounds ridiculous! Your first thought or response is probably something to the extent of who could be this crazy or stupid even? But after you think about it for a while you will probably realize that we all know somebody just like the man in this story. Let's make it real. We all know some people that just like that man in this story, they are drowning, maybe not literally in the sea or ocean, but they are drowning in life! And just like the man in the story, they are not doing anything about it! They are not doing anything to help or save themselves. Their lights are off, and rent is past due. They've received an eviction notice. Their car has been repossessed. And not only are they not working, but pardon my

English, they ain't even looking for a job! And here you are concerned about and trying to help them out. And even though you might not have the money they need, you have the mindset that maybe you can pitch in or help them to develop some type of plan. But here they are telling you, just like the man from the story, "Naw, don't worry about it! I ain't worried. I prayed. I'm trusting and waiting on the Lord! God's gonna work it out! God will save me!" Have you ever heard the saying that your worst enemy is in-a-me? It's true! Sometimes we ourselves become our own worst enemy! More often than not, we get in our own way and block our own blessings! We get so used to being victims instead of victors and it's as if we fight against ourselves and anyone else that tries to help, save, push, or motivate us to get up and take some action, responsibility, and ownership of our lives, conditions, or situations in our lives. Instead of doing something, anything to better our lives, we do nothing! It's as if we become content and complacent in our conditions without contest. If you are reading this now, do me a favor and just say out loud, FIGHT!

Always remember that waiting is not a time or period of doing nothing! In my studying for this sermon, I read an article written by J. Hampton Keathley III titled "Waiting on the Lord," published June 7, 2004, on Bible.Org. In the article, Keathley discusses how waiting involves a negative and a positive. He states, "Perhaps one of the most difficult aspects of waiting is learning to hold the negatives and the positives in proper balance." The negatives and positives he discusses, which are involved in waiting, are associated with passivity and activity. Passivity is defined as acceptance of what happens, without active response or resistance. Keathley explains what I believe to be a critical key and important for us to understand which is, that with waiting there are both things that we should and should not do. He goes on to discuss how these negatives and positives in relation to waiting are intertwined like the strands in a rope which he states that, "When wound together properly give great strength, courage, patience, and endurance."[1]

---

[1]   J. Hampton Keathley, "Waiting on the Lord," Bible.org, June 7, 2004, bible. org/article/waiting-lord.

In speaking on the negatives of waiting, passivity represents the person we just discussed in our story. The person that refuses to move, rejects ideas, help, and passes up opportunities which ultimately cost a person to miss out. Passivity in a negatives state can cost you to miss the peace of God. Passivity and waiting are alike in that apart from God we can do nothing. It's beyond this point that passivity and waiting can take separate paths. A passive person refuses to take action and does nothing when God is clearly leading them onward. In contrast, waiting can be positive in that waiting and trusting are both direct responses that are in line with God's leading. In this example, waiting might mean taking action or it might mean being still. As you may know, sometimes it takes more power to not do something and wait upon the Lord than it does to act hastily, which is often our natural reaction. Waiting enhances our appetite for the good things God has in store for us. Waiting requires us to deny fleshly lusts and to set aside our desire for immediate gratification in some easier way. When you think about your life and periods where you were going through or struggling with something, this is where we often find ourselves not wanting to wait and so you took matters into your own hands looking for some form of instant relief or gratification. But Jesus says any man that wants to follow me let him deny himself and take up his cross and follow me. Waiting is one of the ways that we take up our cross and follow him.

Now let's talk about activity. In dealing with activity or active waiting, waiting involves three things:

(1) Things we do as in doing the right things. This includes such activities as serving, praying, and positioning ourselves.
(2) Things we are not to do as in our reactions such as being anxious, doubtful, and as previously discussed taking matters into our own hands.
(3) Things that happen to us, in us, and for us in the process of biblical waiting.

The book of Isaiah speaks of this in Isaiah 48:10 in which the prophet says:

Behold I have refined thee, but not with silver; I have chosen thee in the furnace of affliction. (Isaiah 48:10 KJV)

This lets us know that we are being refined. Another scripture that supports this is found the book of 1 Peter 1:7 in which the apostle lets us know that:

These trials will show that your faith is genuine. It is being tested as fire tests and purifies gold—though your faith is far more precious than mere gold. So when your faith remains strong through many trials, it will bring you much praise and glory and honor on the day when Jesus Christ is revealed to the whole world. (1 Peter 1:7 NLT)

We all know some people and I hope it's not you, but people that just react to everything that happens or everything that they see! That person that if someone says something to them that they don't like, they just go right off the deep end in anger or hurt. Or what about that coworker who if somebody at the job gets laid off, they get so worried that they literally make themselves sick. I mean they might as well go as far as packing they boxes because they are convinced that they are next. They start calling folks and telling everybody, "You know they laying folks off at work so I don't know what I'm gon' do. I just got this new car I don't know how I'm gon' pay for it!"

Times of waiting on the Lord are designed to be those times when our faith is stretched and our intimacy in our relationship with God is enhanced. Waiting on the Lord is good for us. It helps us to develop patience and endurance. It calls for us to exercise our faith, and it builds our faith in God and in God's promises. It teaches us to trust and to act based on what God has said rather than to always react on what we see. So as the scripture says it teaches us to walk by faith and not by sight! Waiting involves an active seeking, trying, moving, and working to seek God's direction and will while letting his peace rule in our hearts. It is a peace that passes all understanding, and it is worth every trial we endure for it to be refined.

I stated earlier that David was a great example from the Bible of a person that waited well. In fact, David waited for over twenty years to reign over all of Israel. But David's waiting also represented a busy time in his life. In the biblical account of the story of David and Saul, we learn that it was Saul who preceded David as the king of Israel. Saul, however, was not fulfilling his role as the king. For example, as the king, it was Saul's job to protect the city of Keliah. It was also Saul's job to fight against the Philistines. But Saul wasn't doing his job, and so the Lord called David to be the new king. You see God loved his people too much to allow them to suffer at the hands of an unfaithful king, and so if Saul wasn't going to fulfill his responsibility, then God would raise up a man who would. David was that man! Now of course Saul wasn't happy about losing his kingdom, and as a result of this, Saul turned against David and even plotted to have David killed. This would lead to David fleeing from Saul in attempts to save his life, but David did much more than just flee. In the book of 1 Samuel chapter 23, you will read where David delivered the people of Keilah from the Philistines! God had promised David that he would be king, and God directed David to act like a king even if he was not yet king! See right there, somebody needs to get that in their spirit! Sometimes you have to act like you have already got it even when you don't! Sometimes you got to act like you've conquered it even if you're still going through! In Philippians 3:12, the Apostle Paul writes:

> **Not that I have already obtained all this, or have already arrived at my goal, but I press on to take hold of that for which Christ Jesus took hold of me. (Philippians 3:12 NIV)**

You have to act like you got the victory even though inside you might feel defeated! You have to act like you got the victory even when everywhere you look and everything you see looks dark and it looks like it's the end! David said:

Yea, though I walk through the valley of the shadow of death, I will fear no evil: for thou art with me; thy rod and thy staff they comfort me. (Psalm 23:4 KJV)

Have you ever seen a boxing match? For those of you that have, if you watch boxing, then you know that every fight doesn't end with a knockout. So sometimes when there is not a knockout, the fight still may have been one-sided, but because there wasn't a knockout in order to determine the winner of the fight, they have to go to the score cards for a decision. Now, one of the fighters knows that they didn't win! In fact, they know they got their butt whipped! They can feel it throughout their entire body! But that fighter still goes to his corner, and he raises both his arms high above his head to appear like he's still in it! What I'm saying is, sometimes even though you might be going through, Satan might have you on the ropes, and he is whipping your butt. But listen, everybody doesn't have to know! You don't have to look like what you've been or presently might be going through! You can look like you know that you're coming out!

But they that wait upon the LORD shall renew their strength; they shall mount up with wings as eagles; they shall run, and not be weary; and they shall walk, and not faint. (Isaiah 40:31 KJV)

Sometimes you have to act like you're winning! I spent twenty years in corporate America. One of the things they used to always say at my job was that you have to dress for success! You have to dress for the position you want and not the position that you are in. What I'm saying to you today is that you have to think yourself victorious!

You can do it! In fact, I know you can do it because you've done it before. What are you talking about, Pastor? Okay, let me show you. It wasn't that long ago. It's no different than back when before you were saved and found out that Lil Nook Nook was cheating on you with KeKe, and you were just devastated! I mean all week you was just tore up, crying nonstop, wouldn't eat, couldn't sleep, and wouldn't go nowhere. Until finally, your girlfriends called you and came over and got you out of bed. They told you that they weren't leaving until you came with them. Next thing you know, you did your hair and then you put on that dress that looks just like the one you seen Beyonce in, and you went out. You went to the club, and you looked like you were the most available and baddest thing in there! You didn't go looking crazy and tore up from the floor up! So why is it that when Satan got your back against the wall, why come out the house looking like Mrs. Sealy?

David waited well! He acted like he was king even though he wasn't yet. What else did David do? He inquired of the Lord. When the people came to David pleading for his help instead of Saul's, David went to God! In doing so, this shows David's wisdom, godliness, and obedience. David knew who God said he would become, and he waited well! Think about some of us. Think if God would have told some of us what he told David to do. Or just think about when your boss comes to you at work and asks you to do something. What's the first thing you say? "That ain't my job!" "That ain't my responsibility!" Some of you would have told God, "Uh, uh, Saul still the king. Let him deal with it!" You know I ain't lying! Then we wonder why we miss our promotion or blessing. But because David was wise, he inquired of the Lord. He prayed! And when David inquired of the Lord, he was willing to do just as the Lord commanded. This is also important because sometimes when we call on the Lord, our minds are already made up. We already know what we're willing to do. We already know that there are certain things we will do and other things that we won't. I preached a sermon before, and I got the title from a song that some of you will remember from Bobby Caldwell. The title was "What You Won't Do, Do For Love." Am I lying? Is this not how we go to God? "Alright, God, I'm gon' do this but that's it!" "This the last thing I'm gon' do, the last time I'm gon' go and try to talk to so and so. If they don't act right this time, I'm done with them!" Oh, you ain't never done that? Lol! Sometimes me and my wife be upset with each other, and we don't be talking. I know what you are thinking don't judge me, some of y'all do it too! But we be done went back and forth over something one too many times to the extent where one of us has gotten upset or felt disrespected. So she'll go to her corner of the house, and I'll go to mine. Next thing you know, some time be done passed or too much time be done passed. Because you have to be careful with that to not give a foothold to the enemy. So too much time be done passed, and I call myself have calmed down some and prayed. So I might be like, "Okay, God, I'm gon' go back up there and do this, and if she doesn't respond like I think she should or if she still acting a fool, that's it I'm done!" 1-800-Lawyers it is! Lol! But this is what we do, and again, this isn't really inquiring of the Lord at all. David waited well.

Let's talk about others from the Bible who waited well. Noah also waited well. Noah was obedient to what God told him to do even though to everyone else Noah might have looked like a fool. Noah worked building the ark while he waited for it to rain. He worked while he waited for the season to change. Despite what everyone was thinking and saying and despite how crazy he looked to others, God had told him something and he remained unmovable as he waited on the promise of God. What about Jacob? Jacob waited well by working for fourteen years to get the wife Racheal that he wanted. These are all examples of people who not only waited on the Lord but waited well. From their examples, we can learn how we should wait. We should never be like the story of the man drowning. We should never think that while we wait we are to do nothing, unless in fact that's what God told us to do. Otherwise, we ought to be doing something! If Satan is attacking you, if he is stealing your blessings and joy, you have to do something! And although sometimes we may not be able to do what we would most like to do, we can do what God has given us to do while we wait on him to fulfill his promise and purpose. Do you know anybody that won't work at all? I'm talking about a job. Do you know any folks that feel like they are too good to work at McDonald's or some other jobs that they feel are beneath them? Meanwhile, they are drowning! Again, the Word of God says, **"Whatsoever thy hand findeth to do, do it with thy might" (Ecclesiastes 9:10 KJV).** You have to understand that wherever you are now, that doesn't mean that this is the last job you gon' have. But until God blesses you with better, do something! Wait well!

Just as we can look to the Bible for examples of those that waited well, we can also look to the Word of God for examples and consequences for those that didn't wait so well. We can see examples of people that waited with worry and wonder as in doubt. We can see people that waited while whining. Just look at the children of Israel. Through Moses, God was freeing the children of Israel from bondage and leading them out of Egypt and into the Promise Land. But throughout the journey and the time that it was taking for them to reach the promise and the Promise Land, they didn't wait well. The children of Israel were always in doubt. They were always wondering, whining, and complaining. Even though while in the wilderness God had shown them miracle after miracle yet, they still doubted and whined. And because of the way they waited, their consequence or punishment was that they would end up waiting for the rest of their lives having never received the promise of God. They never made it to the Promise Land. They died in the wilderness. You have to be careful about how you wait!

If there is anyone in the Bible who would have had a reason to complain, my vote would go to Job. Job went through a season of tribulation, sorrow, and subtraction where he literally lost everything! Job lost his cattle, children, and his wife who turned against him. Job's body was struck with a skin disease. Again, Job lost everything but never whined nor doubted as he waited on God. He kept trusting and believing. He never took matters into his own hands. He never cursed or sinned against God. He went through his season remaining faithful as he waited on the Lord! As a result of how Job waited, everything he lost he got it all back! Because Job knew how to wait, he got double for his trouble! Job's trials and tribulations should encourage us to be assured knowing that God will make it worth the wait!

As I close, if you want to live fast and die young, if you want everything now or in a hurry, or if you can't wait for anything, if you're one that has to eat in a hurry, you can keep eating at McDonald's going through the drive thru ordering value meals. But my warning to you is that you should know that there is not much nutrition in that! But if you've ever been fortunate enough to experience some finer things in life and you've learned that the "fast life," or in my prior example the McDonald's way, or fast food really is no good for you! If you've been there and done that and had the opportunity to grow and experience better, and so you've decided that you prefer a gourmet meal, then you also have learned and know that you may have to wait a little while. Wisdom has taught us that the reason for the wait is because anything worth having is worth both waiting and working for. Your blessings or the finer things in life don't always happen quickly no matter how Satan may try to convince you otherwise. Just as gourmet meals aren't prepared quickly or easily no matter how good the television commercials make it look. We have become a microwave generation, but I have never once seen or heard of anyone putting food into a microwave because they thought that it would taste better than something that came off the stovetop, oven, or from a Crock-Pot. We use the microwave because it's convenient, and we want to eat fast. We use the microwave because we want it right now. But we use the stovetop, oven, or Crock-Pot when we want to eat well. And so it is with God's plans and promises for you. They are not from the microwave aisle or selection. God slow cooks his plans and his children to bring out the very best in them. Though sometimes it may feel like it's taking too long, you can almost always count on the fact that God will make it worth the wait. You may have heard the saying that God may not come when you want him, but he's always on time! You can also be assured knowing that when it's in God's plan for you to wait, he will always make it worth your wait! I hope I have at least one witness reading this that can help me testify; He's an on-time God, yes, he is!

For our light affliction, which is but for a moment, worketh for us a far more exceed-

ing and eternal weight of glory. (2 Corinthians 4:17 KJV)

For his anger endureth but a moment; in his favour is life: weeping may endure for a night, but joy cometh in the morning. (Psalm 30:5 KJV)

But they that wait upon the LORD shall renew their strength; they shall mount up with wings as eagles; they shall run, and not be weary; and they shall walk, and not faint. (Isaiah 40:31 KJV)

Say this prayer:

Gracious and Heavenly Father, thank you for this word that has broken strongholds in my life. As you know, there are several things and prayer requests that I have been waiting for. Lord, forgive me for my sins. Forgive me for any complaints, doubts, or for any attempts to take matters into my own hands rather than waiting for you. Bless me to wait well, Lord. Bless me to wait like a waiter serving you, Lord. Give me wisdom to know what you would have me to do as I wait, Bless me to know whether I am truly waiting on you or if you are waiting on me. Keep me as I await your answers and blessings! I am trusting you, God. I love you, and I will wait for you knowing that my waiting shall not be in vain! In Jesus's name, amen.

7

◈

Your Gait to Your Gate

This is a sermon that I preached for the sixth anniversary of my home Church Faith Walkers Assembly located in Rockford, Illinois, where my Bishop John F. Senter is the overseer. The theme chosen for the anniversary was faith walking. This sermon takes a look at both words while focusing on the importance of your walk into your destiny.

> **Enter ye in at the strait gate: for wide is the gate, and broad is the way, that leadeth to destruction, and many there be which go in thereat: Because strait is the gate, and narrow is the way, which leadeth unto life, and few there be that find it. (Matthew 7:13–14 KJV)**

As we were blessed to gather and celebrate six years of ministry at Faith Walkers Assembly, the theme that Bishop chose, and we had been talking about all month was faith walking. Two words, the first word being *faith*. Now faith was a word that we had not only discussed for this month or occasion, but as members of Faith Walkers Assembly, faith was a word that every member knew about. In fact, the motto of the church came from 2 Corinthians 5:7 which reads:

> **For we walk by faith, not by sight. (2 Corinthians 5:7 KJV)**

So again, if you were a member of Faith Walkers Assembly, you knew about faith. It had been embedded in us! We knew Hebrews 11:1 which reads:

Now faith is the substance of things hoped for, the evidence of things not seen. (Hebrews 11:1 KJV)

We knew that without faith, it is impossible to please God (Hebrews 11:6). We knew that faith comes by hearing and hearing by the Word of God (Romans 10:17). And we knew that faith without works is dead (James 2:26). Being that we were well versed on faith, what I chose to focus on for my church's anniversary and what I want to focus on through your reading today is the second word, *walking*. Say the word *walk* out loud. Now I want you to take a minute or two and think about this question, "What is you walk like?"

Back in the day, the old school or church folks when describing or talking about an individual they would do so by summarizing or characterizing that person by simply saying, "They walk ain't right." For example, they might say, "Yeah, he or she look and dress nice and they got this or that, but they walk ain't right." I love this because in their words and description lies knowledge and wisdom that comes from many years of experience, which has taught them what's most important in life. Just as wisdom has taught us that you can't judge a book by its cover and that everything that glitters ain't gold, the old school or elders had figured out that above whatever a person might look like or have going for themselves, it was their walk that mattered most!

It's important that we talk about walking today because I am convinced that even the church, the body of Christ, has a walking disorder! We walk weird. We walk funny. Our walk confuses people. We don't walk it like we talk it! If you listen to us, if you didn't know us and you were to just listen to us talk, it would confuse you. It would confuse you because you might hear faith, but when you see our walk, you would notice that the two don't line up. They don't add up. One of my favorite books growing up was *Aesop's Fables*. If you are not familiar with the book, it is a book of fables written by Aesop who was believed to have been a Greek slave and storyteller. In his fables, Aesop uses animals and their natural tendencies to teach lessons of wisdom with regard to human nature. I want to share one of the fables from the book, which I believe serves as a great analogy in what we're reading about today. The fable is called **"The Young Crab and His Mother."**

THE YOUNG CRAB AND HIS MOTHER

"Why in the world do you walk sideways like that?" said a mother crab to her son. "You should always walk straight forward with your toes turned out."

"Show me how to walk, mother dear," answered the little crab obediently, "I want to learn."

So, the old Crab tried and tried to walk straight forward. But she could walk sideways only, like her son. And when she wanted to turn her toes out, she tripped and fell on her nose.

The moral of the story is example is better than preception.

Don't tell others how to act unless you can set a good example.

It's a cute little story, but it reminds me that a lot of people want to be leaders. Even in the church you have a lot of folks who want to lead. People want to be in charge, they want to be a part of leadership. They want a title. But what they don't understand is that you don't lead by a title, you lead by example! I ask you again, "How is your walk?" As kids, we all used to play the game "follow the leader." However, as adults, many of us have never learned to follow. How are you going to lead me if you don't know how to get to where it is that you are trying to go? That's the blind leading the blind. In the Word of God, Jesus asks how can that happen?

**And he spake a parable unto them, Can
the blind lead the blind? shall they not both
fall into the ditch? (Luke 6:39 KJV)**

Now, I don't know about you, but I'm not trying to end up in no ditch. Show me how to walk! I want to learn!

Growing up, some of you may have had parents that used to tell you, "Don't do as I do, do as I say!" I'm sure I have more than one witness reading this who has learned and can testify that this really doesn't work. 'Cause even if you didn't do it back then, for sure that was all the instruction you needed to perfect it later. Through this, we have all grown to learn that actions speak louder than words. Know that your kids and everybody else for that matter, though they might not listen to anything that you say, but best believe they're watching everything you do! The Bible says:

**Train up a child in the way he should go:
and when he is old, he will not depart from it.
(Proverbs 22:6 KJV)**

The training is through your walk. Say out loud, "It's your walk!"

To help us understand the importance of our walk, let's look at some definitions of *walk*.

walk definition

1. **a: to move along on foot: advance by steps.**

From this definition, we can see the purpose of walking. Walking is supposed to advance you. Now of course, we can walk backward, but even so, you cannot walk back in time.

> 2. **to go with (someone) to a place by walking: to walk with (someone).**

I want you to write this question down so that you can think about it later. Who are you walking with?

> 3. **To pursue, to follow a certain course of action or way of life: to conduct oneself/life in a particular manner.**

We can find a couple examples of this in the book of Genesis.

> **And Enoch walked with God: and he was not; for God took him. (Genesis 5:24 KJV)**

> **These are the generations of Noah: Noah was a just man and perfect in his generations, and Noah walked with God. (Genesis 6:9 KJV)**

> 4. **To be or act in association: continue in union**

A scripture that I often quote from the minor prophet Amos asks:

> **Can two walk together, except they be agreed? (Amos 3:3 KJV)**

> 5. **To avoid criminal prosecution or conviction. To be acquitted.**

Now that one right there ought to make you happy! That one ought to make you shout! Has anybody reading this ever been acquitted? If you belong to Christ, you should know that you've been acquitted! David said, "Let the redeemed of the Lord say so!"

Let the redeemed of the LORD say so, whom he hath redeemed from the hand of the enemy. (Psalm 107:2 KJV)

He walked! Because he walked, I can hear Kanye saying, "Because Jesus walked," I walked! Because Jesus walked, we walked! You see, it's not that I wasn't guilty! It's not that I didn't do what they said I did! But Hallelujah praise Jesus for what he did! Praise him because of who he is! I walked! It was covered!

In the physical, you can tell a lot about a person just by observing the way they walk. Some people have a confident walk. Just by looking at them, you can see through their posture and how they hold their head high that they are confident. Or have you ever paid attention to royalty, the king, queen, prince, or princess? They literally walk like their royalty. How about Joe Cool, you know the brother with all the swag, limping, and pimping down the block like he got theme music accompanying him. Likewise, just from the way a person is walking, you can tell if they are down and out or depressed. Their posture is slumped, head hanging low, and shoulders sunk as if they are carrying the weight of the world on their shoulders. Dr. Martin Luther King Jr. had a quote that said, "A man can't ride your back unless it's bent." Fellas, have you ever watched a woman walk? Come on now, I'm talking about before we were saved, of course (lol)! I remember an old school song by Slave called **"Watching You."** Y'all remember that? The lyrics was ***Walking down the street watching ladies go by watching you.***

Yeah! But women are able to change up their walk, and based on how a woman is walking, you can tell if she's sophisticated; and when she wants, she can even walk sexy. From a person's walk, you can tell if they are rushing or in a hurry. You can tell if a person is lost, usually evident by somewhat walking in circles. You can tell if a person is lame, as in handicap or injured. They might walk with a cane or limp. You can tell if a person has bad feet or if their feet are hurting. You can also tell if a person is plotting something or up to no good. They have a sneaky walk. Lastly, you can tell if a person is fearful, worried, or scared. They might be looking around or always looking back as they walk. All these many different things you can tell just by looking at how a person walks.

Let's go back to school for a second. What's the shortest distance between two points? A straight line! In relation to walking, being that we have all these different ways and directions in which we can walk, so that we won't be confused, Jesus makes it clear in which direction or manner we should walk in teaching us.

> **Because strait is the gate, and narrow is the way, which leadeth unto life, and few there be that find it. (Matthew 7:14 KJV)**

As I wrote earlier, walking advances us. Those of us that are able to walk, do so every day. We walk to do our daily activities, to get around and for exercise. With walking being so important to our lives, having a problem walking or a walking disorder can make our daily lives extremely difficult. As I was studying and preparing this sermon, God revealed this to me, and it's very important so I want to make sure that you get this! A persons manner of walking, the pattern of how you walk is called your gait (GAIT). Now, there are a variety of problems or issues that can cause a person to have an abnormal gait and lead to problems with walking. Starting with the physical, so physically some of these include the following:

- **Injuries, diseases, or abnormal development of the muscles or bones of your legs or feet.**
- **Movement disorders such as Parkinson's disease or other diseases such as arthritis or multiple sclerosis.**
- **Vision or balance problems.**

All of these can affect our walk! How we treat a walking problem or disorder is dependent on the cause. Physical therapy, surgery, or mobility aids are all examples that might help. Well, in the spiritual, it's pretty much the same thing. In our spiritual walk, some problems or issues that can cause a person to have an abnormal gait and lead to problems "Faith Walking" include the following:

- **Strongholds, (incorrect thinking patterns such as fear, worry, doubt, defeat, and pride)**
- **Injuries, wounds, and scars.**
- **Infections and diseases (hatred, jealousy, hurt, and unforgiveness).**
- **Vision or balance problems.**

Let's take a deeper look into these. I listed a stronghold as an incorrect thinking pattern.

The simplest way for me to explain and express why strongholds are so vital to our spiritual walk is this. For as a man thinketh in his heart so is he (Proverbs 23:7). So many people have hindered or defeated themselves in life simply because of the way that they think. It's as simple as if you say that you can't then you won't. If you don't believe in yourself, then you're already defeated. If you live in fear and doubt or you're always worried, or if you feel like you're cursed or not deserving, or vice versa if you think too highly of yourself to the point that you have foolish pride, all of these can impact your walk. Most importantly, if we're going to walk with God, then we must always be sure that our thoughts line up with God's will. To further complicate this, we have an adversary in Satan who is constantly waging war by planting seeds in his mission to create more strongholds that hinder our walk. The Apostle Paul teaches us about this spiritual warfare in 2 Corinthians 10:3–5:

> **For though we walk in the flesh, we do not war after the flesh: (For the weapons of our warfare are not carnal, but mighty through God to the pulling down of strong holds);**

Casting down imaginations, and every high thing that exalteth itself against the knowledge of God, and bringing into captivity every thought to the obedience of Christ. (2 Corinthians 10:3–5 KJV)

The next problem or issue related to our spiritual or faith walk that can cause us to have an abnormal gait are injuries. Being that we've all experienced physical injuries, I won't spend a lot of time discussing it as we should all be pretty familiar. An injury is simply defined as having damage to the body. This damage could have been caused by an accident, fall, or by being struck with a weapon. Again, as I am sure that we have all experienced, these injuries can result in cuts, wounds, scabs, and scars, which can hinder or cause one to have an abnormal gait. When thinking about and dealing with spiritual injuries, it's pretty much the same thing. Spiritual injuries would be defined as having damage to the spirit. We've all been hurt, wounded, and even struck in our spirit. We've all fallen down not just physically but in our spirit. So many of us have never gotten back up or fully recovered in our spirit. So many of us have never recovered and are still in fact suffering from the cuts, wounds, scabs, and scars, which still remain from our injuries. The damage that you may have suffered from your childhood scarred you, and ever since suffering that injury, your walk has been hindered. Your gait has been abnormal. That person that injured or hurt you whether accidently or on purpose, they cut or scarred you, thus impacting your spiritual walk ever since. This injury has caused you to no longer trust anyone. This injury has caused you to no longer believe. The scab that remains now serves as a defense or wall that no longer allows you to open yourself up to others. Your gait is abnormal to the point that you walk by sight and fear and not by faith.

Let's move on to infections. The definition of *infection* is the process of bacteria or viruses invading the body or making someone ill or diseased (yourdictionary.com). Two examples of the most common viral infections would be the common cold and flu. An example of a bacterial infection would be strep throat. What's important for us to know when it comes to infections and infectious diseases is that many infectious diseases are contagious. Again, I'm sure that we are all familiar with and can recall having an infection at some point in our lives. You can probably recall how bad it made you feel and perhaps even who you got it from.

Having experienced this feeling, as a society, we've all learned to be cautious in efforts to avoid or minimize our chances of catching this infection again. We take certain precautions, such as getting a flu shot yearly and avoiding people that we know have infections. In dealing with spiritual infections, however, the problem is that the symptoms are not as easily identified. It's not a cough, fever, or sore throat that define this infectious disease. This disease is rooted in the heart. These carriers suffer from infections such as hurt, hatred, envy, bitterness, and unforgiveness. Have you ever had an infection and you didn't know it?

Have you ever just been tired and weak to the point that you didn't feel like doing anything? I mean physically you were okay, you didn't have a cough or fever, but you just felt exhausted and couldn't figure out why? Many of us are unknowingly walking around with infections. You've been trying your best to move forward. You've been trying your best to progress, to advance. You've been trying to get back up. You've been trying to get back on your feet, and you haven't been able to figure out why it's been so hard. You might have an infection! Again, all of us at some point in time and most likely multiple times, we've either been affected, or we've been infected by others. When I say others, I'm talking others as in our friends and family, those we walk with, side by side. Those we associate and surround ourselves with. Those who prayed for and encouraged us. Those who believed in us. Those who told us that we can make it. Others also includes the haters, naysayers, and dream killers. The ones that told you that you couldn't do it. The ones that prayed for your downfall. Again, we all either affect or infect others! To affect means to influence or change, to make a difference to. To infect means to contaminate or corrupt. Take thirty seconds and think about whether your walk affects or infects others.

Let your light so shine before men, that they
may see your good works, and glorify your Father
which is in heaven. **(Matthew 5:16 KJV)**

The next issue I'll discuss that can cause a person to have an abnormal gait and lead to problems "Faith Walking" is vision. Vision, how well you can see directly affects your walk! Your walk or gait either adversely or auspiciously not only affects but in fact determines your destination! It determines your destiny! Are you walking by faith or by sight? Check your vision! How far can you see? God told Abram, "As far as you can see you can have!"

Look around from where you are, to the north and south, to the east and west. All the land that you see I will give to you and your off-spring forever. I will make your offspring like the dust of the earth, so that if anyone could count the dust, then your offspring could be counted. Go, walk through the length and breadth of the land, for I am giving it to you. (Genesis 13:14–17 NIV)

Again, I'll ask, how far can you see? Vision is so important to our walk! Not only with regard to how far you can see but also in regard to which direction that you're looking! The enemy can only attack us in our past! He has no power or control over your future or destiny, so he tries to get us to look at our past! He wants you to look backward as you walk! He wants you to look back in attempts to hinder your walk. To give you an abnormal gait. He wants you to focus more on where you come from rather than where you're going! "Ain't that Toya, the one that used to be on crack?" "Ain't that Jerome, the one that went to prison for all them years?" "Ain't that the lady that lost all her kids?" "Ain't that Joseph and Mary's boy, the carpenter?" The enemy wants to remind us of our past and what we did. He wants to keep us looking back so that we begin to doubt where were going! The enemy plants seeds of doubt and begins to question us.

"How you gon' ask God for that?" "How you think you deserve that?" "You know what you did!" "How you think you gon' walk in that church?" "Them folks know your reputation!" "How you think God called you to do that?"

It's that doubt and fear that keeps many of us from walking in our purpose and into our destiny! It's that doubt and fear that keeps us sitting on our gifts! You have a gift! You have purpose! You are chosen! Every one of us in the Body of Christ is important! The Bible says one body many members! The foot can't say to the hand, the ear can't say to the eye, the head can't say to the feet. Read 1 Corinthians 12, the Apostle Paul teaches us that there is no division of the body! We all got a past! We are all ex-somethings! Even in the Bible, before he was Paul, he was Saul. We all know about Saul's walk. Saul walked one way on the road to Damascus, but when he met, God his walk changed! God can turn a test into a testimony! God can turn a mess into a message or even a messenger! When you walk, don't look back! Don't look back! When the angels of God rescued Lot and his family from Sodom and Gomorrah, they gave instructions. They told Lot and his family not to look back. Lot's wife didn't listen; she looked back, and when she did, what happened? She got salty! When you hold on to your history, you do it at the expense of your destiny.

What about Peter's walk? If you can recall, Peter walked on water! Didn't he do it? I mean, he literally walked on water! Last time I checked, that's not normal! When was the last time you walked on water? That was a miracle! Peter performed a miracle! He walked on water, and he did it until he looked around! He did it until he took his focus off Jesus! He looked at the high waves and the wind, and he became afraid and began to sink! But just think what you could do if you kept your focus on God! Just think what you could do if you didn't allow yourself to get distracted by what you see, by all the distractions and wiles that the enemy throws at us. Just to get our attention! Just to get you to take your focus off God! Think what you could do if you truly walked by faith and not by sight! Jesus said greater works shall you do! Praise God! Glory to God! We walk by faith and not by sight!

Think about the blind! People that are blind don't walk like we do. Blind people walk but they don't walk by sight. We see, but even though we can physically see the troubles all around us, haters hating on you, folks lying on you, people all around you going through trials and tribulations, folks giving up, folks falling off, even though everything around us might be falling down, we have to be like David. David said:

> **A thousand shall fall at thy side, and ten thousand at thy right hand; but it shall not come nigh thee. (Psalm 91:7 KJV)**

David said:

> **Yea, though I walk through the valley of the shadow of death, I will fear no evil: for thou art with me; thy rod and thy staff they comfort me. Thou preparest a table before me in the presence of mine enemies. (Psalm 23:4–5 KJV)**

Where? Where did God prepare a table before him? It was in the presence of his enemies! Do you see that? In the presence of my enemies. So they was there! His enemies, his haters, the naysayers, the folks that tried to stop you, all the folks that counted you out, that gave up on you, the folks that told you you wouldn't be here today, they was there! They were in his presence, which means he could see them! But don't let that stop you! You can't let that stop you! You gotta keep walking! You gotta keep walking! Don't worry about that! Don't worry about them over there! Just keep walking! Just keep walking! I ain't blind so I see! And yeah, you'll see! Just like when I preached this, I saw some in the pews! I seen them! I heard what they was saying about me! But you can't worry about that, you gotta keep walking! You gotta keep walking! You gotta walk that thing out! Right now, say out loud, "Walk it out!" You gotta keep walking! You gotta keep walking! You got somewhere to be! God's calling you! You got a destination! You got a destination and a destiny! So I see you! I see you, Satan! I see you, hater! Again, you ain't blind so you'll see him, but you have to keep walking and in situations like this it would be better for us to walk by faith and not by sight! It would be better because what you might be seeing, it's a mess! What you're seeing might look impossible! It might look like there's no way out! What you're seeing, the late Michael Jackson said, "It's too high to get over, too low to get under, you stuck in middle and the pain is thunder!" The devil always wanna be starting something!

I been there! I know how you feel! I've seen what you're seeing! I know how it looks! But if you could just close your eyes! If you could just go blind for a second! If you could just silence the distractions, doubts, and voices in your head! If you could just be like Peter for a moment and walk by faith, it would help you to make it through!

> **And I will bring the blind by a way that they knew not; I will lead them in paths that they have not known: I will make darkness light before them, and crooked things straight. These things will I do unto them, and not forsake them. (Isaiah 42:16 KJV)**

Walking by faith ushers you through. Walking by faith ushers you through the storms and troubled waters. Walking by faith got Shadrack, Meshack, and Abednego through the fiery furnace.

The last issue I'll discuss that can cause a person to have an abnormal gait and lead to problems "Faith Walking" is abnormal development. Abnormal development specifically of your muscles, bones, legs, and feet can lead to injury and diseases. One of the major influences we can control in our development is what we put into our bodies. This not only includes what we feed our physical body but also what we feed our Spirit! Now I like to eat! And when I eat, I like my sides. I like macaroni and cheese, rice, green vegetables, and almost any kind of potatoes. Now as much as I like my sides, I still have to have my meat! I don't get full off the sides! I always make sure I save room 'cause I know it's still some meat, and I don't know about you; but for me, the meat makes the meal! Some folks eat spaghetti as a full meal. I actually just learned this some years ago! I never did that! I mean I eat spaghetti, but I gotta have some catfish or fried chicken somewhere on that plate! For me, spaghetti was always a side! I'm not getting off track with talking about food, but I said that to say this; when it comes to what you feed your spirit, some people need to stick with the entrée and get over the sides!

At the start of this sermon, I wrote that I preached this sermon at my home church, Faith Walkers Assembly, where my Bishop John F. Senter presides. Now for those of you that don't know him, let me tell you that when it comes to feeding his flock, this man of God is a master chef! Faith Walkers Assembly is blessed with an anointed, preaching, teaching, gifted man of God who consistently serves up some marinated, seasoned, tender, juicy, melt-in-your-mouth meat! Y'all remember the movie *Last Friday*? I'm talking about some Brothers BBQ so good it makes you wanna smack your mama! With that said, I can remember back when I was the lead deacon at Faith Walkers Assembly, and we had some I guess "big names" that led the praise team along with some "big name" musicians. During this time, there were some folks that was coming to church just for the music! They were coming to sing and dance! We had people joining the church just to be a part of what was going on! I would often work at the front door as a greeter as well as for security, and so I witnessed where people would come in and take a peek, and if the "big name" musician wasn't singing that week, they would leave! Boy did this bother me! I couldn't understand it! I mean I have nothing against music, and there's nothing wrong with praise, worship, singing, and dancing. Just like there was nothing wrong with Bishop's vision. Bishop wanted five-star service! He wanted folks to have a five-star experience from the parking lot to the benediction, and there was nothing wrong with that! But it was something wrong with the people! The walking disorder that the church has today is because it's something wrong with the people! What I couldn't understand was the mind of the people! You don't come to church for the sides!

Have you ever been to Texas De Brazil, Brazzaz, Fogo De Chao, or any of the other Brazilian steak houses? These restaurants serve some of the best cuts of meat you can think of! I'm talking sausage, steak, top or bottom sirloin, garlic steak, chicken wrapped in bacon, lamb chops, you name it! You don't go there for the sides! I mean, yeah, they have sides, but who goes to a steakhouse for sides? I don't understand that! You need meat! Your spirit needs meat! That meat helps your walk! That mean strengthens your bones! That meat gets in your spirit! David said:

> **Thy word have I hid in mine heart, that I might not sin against thee. (Psalm 119:11 KJV)**

You need his word!

> **Thy word is a lamp unto my feet, and a light unto my path. (Psalm 119:105 KJV)**

Thank God for the first gospel singer! Thank God for Gospel music! Because some folks that's the only word y'all get! That's all y'all retain! If it's got a beat and some drums, that's the only way y'all can eat it! Like children, that's your fast food!

JESUS WILL WORK IT OUT!

IT'S THE GOD IN ME!

MAKES ME CLAP MY HANDS MAKE ME WANNA DANCE, SHOUT!

Your development is abnormal along with your walk because of what you have been feeding your spirit. Paul talks about this in Hebrews 5, and I want to share this from the living version as it reads so clear, but Paul tells the church:

> **You have been Christians a long time now, and you ought to be teaching others, but instead you have dropped back to the place where you need someone to teach you all over again the very first principles in God's Word. You are like babies who can drink only milk, not old enough for solid food. And when a person is still living on milk it shows he isn't very far along in the Christian life and doesn't know much about the difference between right and wrong. He is still a baby Christian! You**

will never be able to eat solid spiritual food and understand the deeper things of God's Word until you become better Christians and learn right from wrong by practicing doing right. (Hebrews 5:12–13 TLB)

It's sad to say, but if it wasn't for gospel music, some Christians wouldn't be able to quote a scripture! You wouldn't be able to recite a scripture! I ain't lying! So this what folks do, this is how they walk when they going through something or when they under attack from the enemy. They turn to music for comfort, to make them feel better! They turn to music to make them feel like they're not alone. I'm talking about all music—Luther, Shirley Murdock, Keisha Cole, Mary J Blige, Tupac, Lil Wayne. Whoever you may prefer? Because we've all done it, and the scary thing is, it works! Y'all know it works! It comforts you! It gets you through the night! You lay there and you cry yourself to sleep! You cry till you can't cry no more, till you're all cried out (which is also a song)! And so you believe its okay. But the problem is its abnormal development! It's a walking disorder! It's two steps forward and two steps back. That gets you nowhere! That only works in the club! (Cha-cha now!) Some folks walk doing a two-step, side to side, straddling the fence, unstable in all your ways! You gotta get your club walk outta here! That's why music is so important to some because it's what you relate to and what grabs you. It's what you associate with and what you know. But does it deliver you? Does it save you? Does it stop the attack of the enemy? Does it stop the devil in his tracks? Does it get Satan up off you? And does it advance you?

Earlier, I gave you some definitions of walk. How are you walking? Who are you walking with? Are you walking by faith or by sight? Are you walking with God, or are you walking with Mary J Blige? Are you walking with Jay-Z? If you'll listen, you'll hear how folks be sounding crazy! In regard to music folks, be looking and sounding crazy! All these superfans and groupies out here following an artist all over the country. Folks jumping up and down, screaming and passing out all because Beyonce touched you! Folks be talking about I never would have made it through my situation without Whitney! Or me and Mary J, we got through that one together! Is you crazy? Folks got lights on, nobody home! It's literally idol worship! We might not mean it to be, but it's another form of idol worship! Glorifying idols and man, as if God, Jesus Christ, and his Holy Spirit was not sufficient! That wasn't enough, it took Barry White or Rihanna to get you through! Who are you walking with? You better be walking with God! God is the only one that's surefire! God is the only one that guarantees you the victory!

> **Ye are of God, little children, and have overcome them: because greater is he that is in you, than he that is in the world. (1 John 4:4 KJV)**

> **I was young and now I am old, yet I have never seen the righteous forsaken or their children begging bread. (Psalm 37:25 NIV)**

> **I can do all things through Christ which strengtheneth me. (Philippians 4:13 KJV)**

> **Casting all your care upon him; for he careth for you. (1 Peter 5:7 KJV)**

> **Come to me, all you who are weary and burdened, and I will give you rest. Take my yoke upon you and learn from me, for I am gentle and humble in heart, and you will find rest for your souls. For my yoke is easy and my burden is light. (Matthew 11:28–30 NIV)**

How is your walk? How are you walking? Who are you walking with? Think about when Jesus was under attack and led into the wilderness to be tempted by Satan. How did he walk? How did he stand? How did he advance? Who did he walk with? I'll tell you! He walked by the word! He stood on the word! Jesus didn't start singing to Satan! That only works in cartoons, you know when you see the serpent dancing to the sound of the flute! That doesn't work in real life! Jesus showed us how to walk! Jesus said:

> **It is written, Man shall not live by bread alone, but by every word that proceedeth out of the mouth of God. (Matthew 4:4 KJV)**

He put the word on him! Jesus put the word on the enemy three times and the enemy departed! As promised in the word:

> **Submit yourselves therefore to God. Resist the devil, and he will flee from you. (James 4:7 KJV)**

> **Humble yourselves therefore under the mighty hand of God, that he may exalt you in due time: Casting all your care upon him; for he careth for you. Be sober, be vigilant; because your adversary the devil, as a roaring lion, walketh about, seeking whom he may devour. (1 Peter 5:6–8 KJV)**

> **(For the weapons of our warfare are not carnal, but mighty through God to the pulling down of strong holds;) Casting down imaginations, and every high thing that exalteth itself against the knowledge of God, and bringing into captivity every thought to the obedience of Christ. (2 Corinthians 10:4–5 KJV)**

Again, I ask you, how is your walk? Say out loud, "Walk it out!" Yes, you gotta walk it out! You gotta get your walk right! You gotta learn how to walk! You gotta know who you are walking with! You gotta know how to stand! You gotta know how to fight! You gotta know when to walk! Why? Because as Bishop John Senter still often says to his flock, God is still looking for faith walkers! Yes, he's still looking! Are you out there? Are there any faith walkers reading this? Bishop's declaration is not just for the members of Faith Walkers Assembly, it's for all of us! If you're going to be a part of the body, you must always remember that there's only one body of Christ! Many members but one body! The true church! If you're going to be a part of the body, then you have to learn how to walk! You have to learn how to advance the kingdom! You have to become a faith walker! Stop walking based on your emotional state or how you're feeling! H-Town had a song back in the day where they sang, "Emotions make you cry sometimes!" Stop walking based off how things look or what you're seeing. These are all the wiles and distractions that the enemy throws at us to get you to change your focus, direction, and walk! Walk by faith and not by sight! Walk by faith at all times through whatever situation, trials, and tribulations and keep your focus on Jesus. Keep your head to the sky despite whatever it is that keeps you walking straight! I saved my sermon title until the end: "YOUR GAIT TO YOUR GATE"!

Ultimately, it's your walk that will determine where you enter. Your gait will determine your gate!

Enter ye in at the strait gate: for wide is the gate, and broad is the way, that leadeth to destruction, and many there be which go in thereat: Because strait is the gate, and narrow is the way, which leadeth unto life, and few there be that find it. (Matthew 7:13–14 KJV)

Say this prayer:

Gracious and Heavenly Father, teach me how to walk. By faith and not by sight. By your will and not mine. Teach me to walk without any fear, doubt, or hesitation. Heal me from any hurts, infections, or injuries that may have hindered me. Order my steps, Lord. In your

word, in your path, in your plans for my life. Don't let me wander or walk into the wilderness. Don't allow the enemy to lead me astray. Don't let me look back. Don't allow me to be distracted by the high winds or waves. Keep my mind and vision stayed on you. Let me walk after the examples that you gave in your word. Correct my gait so that I may one day enter into your gate. As the old hymn that the church used to sing, Lord, lead me, guide me along your way, for if you lead me, I cannot stray. Lord, let me walk each day with thee. Lead me, Oh Lord, lead me. In Jesus's name, amen.

8

Exodus 16
The Message in the Manna

God is always speaking! Whether it be through his word, actions, mercy, or grace, God is always teaching and guiding us along his path and plans for our lives. The word of God says that, "All Scripture is God-breathed and is useful for teaching, rebuking, correcting and training in righteousness, so that the servant of God may be thoroughly equipped for every good work" (2 Timothy 3:16–17 NIV). The problem is that for a multitude of reasons, we often miss God's message. We expect God to answer or respond to our circumstances or prayer request in a preconceived manner based on our understanding. But again, God tells us that, "For as the heavens are higher than the earth, so are my ways higher than your ways, and my thoughts than your thoughts" (Isaiah 55:9 KJV). This sermon looks at the biblical record and exodus of the children of Israel and reminds us how especially during our most critical times of need not to miss the message from God!

Our sermon and lesson for this chapter comes from the Old Testament in the book of Exodus. The word Exodus translates from the Greek work *Exodos*, which means going out. Already that's some good news for somebody reading this right now! If you believe me, somebody shout it like Diana Ross, say, "I'm coming out!" The book of Exodus details God's call to the children of Israel who we know as God's chosen people. God's call to his chosen people was a call to get up and leave from their current position of bondage and slavery they were suffering in Egypt under the rule of Pharoah. To give you a little background into how the children of Israel had become slaves, the children of Israel were descendants of Abraham and the slavery they were facing had been prophesized to Abraham in the book of Genesis. In Genesis chapter 15:13, God tells Abraham:

> **Then the LORD said to him, "Know for certain that for four hundred years your descendants will be strangers in a country not their own and that they will be enslaved and mistreated there." (Genesis 15:13 NIV)**

I want you to make a side note right here. I want you to note this scripture as proof that God allows some things to happen in our lives that might not feel so good! God will allow some folks to mistreat you! He will allow some people to hurt you! God will allow some folks to turn their backs on you! And just as with the children of Israel, God will even allow some folks to oppress you! He allows some things to happen in our lives that might not seem to be good for us. But you have to remember, in fact you have to remind yourself that, "All things work together for good to them that love God, to them who are called according to his purpose" (Romans 8:28 KJV). And so again God told Abraham, "Know for certain that for four hundred years your descendants will be strangers in a country not their own and that they will be enslaved and mistreated there" (Genesis 15:13 NIV). But in verse 14, God says:

> **But I will punish the nation they serve as slaves, and afterward they will come out with great possessions. (Genesis 15:14 NIV)**

Somebody shout out loud, "Afterward!" Whatever situation that you might be suffering through right now, I want you to know that God has promised you an afterward!

In reading the book of Exodus, you will learn how God rescues and delivers his chosen people by guiding them through the Red Sea, into the desert, and eventually by bringing them to Mount Sinai in the Sinai Peninsula. It is in Mount Sinai where God institutes his system of laws we know as the Ten Commandments. God also gives his chosen people instructions in worship and establishes them as the nation of Israel. From this, we can see that the book of Exodus is a book of great spiritual significance. There are also several significant themes and comparisons throughout the book of Exodus. For example, in the book of Exodus, Israel's slavery also serves as a picture or comparison of man's slavery to sin. Just like Israel, we too were once in bondage! Just like Israel though, we were chosen by God. We were also once slaves to sin! Sin both had and ruled over us! It is only through God's grace and mercy! It is only through God's divine plan and through faith in our sacrificial lamb Jesus Christ, through his obedience, leadership, and guidance, that we were able to escape our slavery to sin. Glory to God!

When reading the book of Exodus, you will see that God leads and directs the people of Israel through the leadership of Moses. In comparison today, God also leads us into freedom and truth through Jesus and the Holy Spirit. Today, God leads us through wisdom, wise leadership, and through preaching and teaching of his word. His word says in Romans 10:17:

So then faith cometh by hearing, and hearing by the word of God. (Romans 10:17 KJV)

Before reconciling this, just a few verses prior the author Paul ask,

How then shall they call on him in whom they have not believed? and how shall they believe in him of whom they have not heard? and how shall they hear without a preacher? (Romans 10:14 KJV)

As a pastor, I have taught and preached about the children of Israel several times before. I have talked about how the children of Israel were a murmuring, fearful, doubtful, whining, and complaining people! The children of Israel seemed to never be satisfied. They were always asking for more and constantly rebelling against God. When studying the children of Israel, you might ask yourself, "Why did God choose them?" But in keeping it real with yourself, you might also wonder or ask God, "Lord, why did you choose me?" I mean, honestly, are we much better than them? They say that you should learn from your elders and ancestors. Each generation should learn from the generation that came before. Well in looking to the Word of God and at the children of Israel, there is much that we can learn!

The first point we can learn from the children of Israel is that although they were often complaining, rebellious, and sinning against God, God loved them! God loved them just like he loves you! In the book of Exodus, you will read how God would discipline and punish the children of Israel. God would allow then to go through sufferings. Wisdom speaks to us through Proverbs 3:11–12, which reads:

My son, do not despise the LORD's discipline, and do not resent his rebuke, because the LORD disciplines those he loves, as a father the son he delights in. (Proverbs 3:11–12 NIV)

But even though God would discipline and allow them to go through sufferings, God would also continue to show them mercy! Time and time again, the children of Israel would turn away from God; and as a result, he would punish them. But once they returned to him, time and time again he would hear their cry. There are several examples in the book of Exodus where the children of Israel were crying out to God for deliverance, and because God loved them and was concerned about them, he rescued them!

The LORD said, "I have indeed seen the misery of my people in Egypt. I have heard

*them crying out because of their slave drivers,
and I am concerned about their suffering. So I
have come down to rescue them from the hand
of the Egyptians and to bring them up out of
that land into a good and spacious land, a
land flowing with milk and honey... And now
the cry of the Israelites has reached me, and I
have seen the way the Egyptians are oppressing
them. So now, go. I am sending you to Pharaoh
to bring my people the Israelites out of Egypt."*
(Exodus 3:7–10 NIV)

Somebody reading this you ought to say, "Thank you, God!" Somebody reading this right now you ought to start praising God! You ought to thank God for his word! You ought to thank God for his promise! God's promise to the children of Israel is the same promise God has spoken to you! Whatever it is that you might be going through today. Whatever it is that has you bound! Whatever misery you might be suffering, God has seen your misery and heard your cry! He has come down to rescue and answer you and the answer is Jesus! Do you know who Jesus is? If you don't know who Jesus is, let me tell you! He's the alpha and the omega!

**"I am the Alpha and the Omega, the
Beginning and the End," says the Lord God.
"I am the God who is, and who was, and who
will come. I am the Mighty One." (Revelation
1:8 NIRV)**

He's the way!

**Jesus saith unto him, I am the way, the
truth, and the life: no man cometh unto the
Father, but by me. (John 14:6 KJV)**

And he is a deliverer!

The thief cometh not, but for to steal, and to kill, and to destroy: I am come that they might have life, and that they might have it more abundantly. (John 10:10 KJV)

So in the same way that God had chosen Israel and had plans to deliver them from Pharaoh and bring them to a land of abundance, a land of milk and honey, God has plans for you! Just like the children of Israel who suffered bondage, slavery, and wandered through the wilderness crying out to God, somebody reading this right now has been doing the same! You've been struggling! You've been carrying this burden! You've been wandering in your own wilderness for far too long! You've been crying out to God! I wrote this sermon to prophesy to you just like the prophet Isaiah prophesized.

The Lord says, "Your request has come at a favorable time." (Isaiah 49:8 TLB)

There is a message in the manna! Let's read from Exodus 16.

The whole Israelite community set out from Elim and came to the Desert of Sin, which is between Elim and Sinai, on the fifteenth day of the second month after they had come out of Egypt. In the desert the whole community grumbled against Moses and Aaron. The Israelites said to them, "If only we had died by the LORD's hand in Egypt! There we sat around pots of meat and ate all the food we wanted, but you have brought us out into this desert to starve this entire assembly to death." (Exodus 16:1–3 NIV)

So here they are, here we see the children of Israel grumbling and complaining! Even after God had brought them out of bondage and slavery, even after God had shown them miracle after miracle. In fact, the book of Exodus records more miracles of God than any other book in the Old Testament. Not to mention the plagues he put on Egypt and Pharaoh including locust, contaminating the water, and killing off all of the firstborn, forcing Pharaoh to make them leave. We're reading and studying from Exodus chapter 16 today, but if you were to go back just one chapter to Exodus 15, you'll read of how the children of Israel were in the desert and had traveled for three days without water, and when they finally came to Marah, they couldn't drink the water because it was bitter. And so again they murmured and complained, and God had Moses to throw a piece of wood in the water and the water became fit to drink! Literally miracle after miracle! Not only for the children of Israel but just like he's done for you and me! "Hold on, I don't think I heard you!" Has he not proven himself to be faithful? But yet here they are, complaining, looking only at what they don't have! Not thinking about where God has just brought them from and in fact saying that they were better off where they were as slaves to Pharaoh! This is what fear does! Let me say that again, this is what fear does! Fear stops you from progressing! Fear stops you from reaching your promised land! Fear stops you dead in your tracks! Fear paralyzes you! Fear infects you! It infects you to the point that you deny God! Fear infects you to the point that you forfeit and surrender your blessings and submit to Satan's plan! Fear is a faith killer! Once your faith is gone, once you have no faith, you have nothing!

> **But without faith it is impossible to please him: for he that cometh to God must believe that he is, and that he is a rewarder of them that diligently seek him. (Hebrews 11:6 KJV)**

The children of Israel were in a dry place, literally! They were in a desert! They weren't in a good situation or so they thought. Just like you think you might not be in a good situation. You might be in a dead-end job. You might be in a relationship that you know isn't going anywhere, yet you won't leave! And so, God makes it worse! He makes it intolerable! He stirs up the nest! Just like a mother bird or eagle does. The same nest that she builds and lays her eggs in. The same nest where her newborn chic's receive comfort, care, and everything they need to grow. But once those babies reach flying age, the mother eagle has to make the only home those babies have ever known uncomfortable. And so, she stirs up the nest not to punish them but rather to motivate them to fly and even learn to soar! In the same way, God stirs up your nest until you have no choice but to leave! And so here we are where finally the children of Israel left. Now, maybe when they left, they expected everything to go smoothly. I'm sure somebody reading this can testify that when you left that bad situation you thought it was sure to get better. Just like a lot of people when they first came to church or gave their life to God and got saved, they might have thought that all their problems would end. You thought that Satan was gone finally just leave you alone and let you be! Well, I'm sorry! I apologize if you thought that! I sincerely apologize if someone led you to believe this! No, you are still going to have your trials! You are still going to have some troubles! And you are still going to have some tests! Folks that were hating on you, they still gon' hate on you, maybe even more! Them folks and demons that was attacking you, they ain't gon' stop attacking you just because you joined church! They ain't gon' stop just because you got saved! Do you remember Job? The Bible records that Job was a just man! Job was favored by God! God put Satan on Job! God asked Satan, "Have you considered my servant Job?"

Then the LORD said to Satan, "Have you considered my servant Job? There is no one on earth like him; he is blameless and upright, a man who fears God and shuns evil." (Job 1:8 NIV)

This shows us that God will still test your faith! God will allow you to be attacked! He will allow you to be tested! Like we see with the children of Israel God will take you through the wilderness! So know that in between your Egypt and your Promise Land, in between your deliverance and your destiny, you will have some ups and downs! This reminds me of a song they used to sing back in the old church called **"I Won't Complain."** You should pull it up on you tube or Pandora or whatever you use listen to, but I can hear the Reverend Paul Jones sing:

I've had some good days
I've had some hills to climb
I've has some weary days
And some lonely nights
But when I look around
And I think things over
All of my good days
Out-weigh my bad days
I won't complain

Glory! Listen, you'll have some days where you feel like stopping! You'll have some days when you feel like giving up! You'll have some days when just like the children of Israel you'll feel like going back! That's why God created manna! Take a second right now to thank God for manna! I want you to say it out loud to yourself say, "Thank God for manna!" Just a little manna!

> **Then the LORD said to Moses, "I will rain down bread from heaven for you. The people are to go out each day and gather enough for that day. In this way I will test them and see whether they will follow my instructions." (Exodus 16:4 NIV)**

I want to talk more about this manna specifically regarding the message in the manna. From the verse above, the first observation we can make is that manna comes from heaven! To minister to the children of Israel and their physical needs, God sent something called "manna" or bread down from heaven. We should not overlook that this is another example of one of the many miracles found in the book of Exodus. It was a miracle of God that bread came down out of heaven for the children of Israel to eat. The children of Israel didn't plant anything! They didn't sow anything! They didn't go anywhere and buy anything to eat! It didn't come from Egypt, and they didn't produce or manufacture it in the wilderness. It was something that God sent down of his own accord! They didn't pray for it. God knew they needed it, and he supplied their need! It's also important to point out that the children of Israel didn't deserve the manna! I mean read the passage; do you see anything that they did to deserve it? All they did was complain and murmur along with continue to display a rebellious attitude and spirit toward the will of God. But thank God for his grace and mercy! God willed to show grace, mercy, patience, kindness, and love to them. Just as he's done the same for you and me!

The next observation I want to point out regarding this manna is that it fell in the wilderness. This shows us that it is not necessary to have the perfect or even ideal conditions for God to work! God didn't need the perfect conditions for manna to fall! God is independent! God is God all alone! He can do whatever he wants whenever he wants! I should have a witness reading this! Somebody reading this should be able to testify! You got the job even though you didn't have all the qualifications! You got the loan even though your credit said that you couldn't get it! God doesn't need perfect conditions in your life to work it out!

What other message, or what else can we see through the manna? How about the fact that it came down from heaven to where they were. They did not have to make a long journey to get to the manna. They did not have to go on a scavenger hunt to find it. There were no mountains to climb or rivers to cross. They didn't have to call UPS or FedEx to schedule a delivery and track it. They did not have to go anywhere to get what they needed. It was easily accessible. It fell all over the ground right outside of their tents and campground. As the great Gospel singer Squire Parsons wrote, "When I could not go to where he was, he came to me." Praise God!

Continuing…

> **The people are to go out each day and gather enough for that day. In this way I will test them and see whether they will follow my instructions. (Exodus 16:4 NIV)**

This is important. God gave specific instructions to the children of Israel regarding the manna, which represents the blessing that he supplied to them. In the same way, the Holy Bible, the Word of God, gives us specific instructions on how we should handle each blessing he supplies us with. God stated that they were only to gather what they needed, enough for that day! He didn't want them trying to store up! God wanted them to depend on him daily!

> **Do not store up for yourselves treasures on earth, where moths and vermin destroy, and where thieves break in and steal. But store up for yourselves treasures in heaven, where moths and vermin do not destroy, and where thieves do not break in and steal. For where your treasure is, there your heart will be also. (Matthew 6:19–21 NIV)**

Why continue to live only on yesterday's blessings? This is exactly what many of us are doing. We are living off on nouns! When I say nouns, I'm talking about persons, places, and things that God may have once blessed or supplied us with for a reason or season that we continue to hold on to or go back and look for God to bless you for a lifetime! You're storing up when God has more!

> **It is of the LORD's mercies that we are not consumed, because his compassions fail not. They are new every morning: great is thy faithfulness. (Lamentations 3:22–23 KJV)**

It is God's will that we have something fresh every day! Fresh manna was to be gathered every day!

Continuing…

> **The people are to go out each day and gather enough for that day. In this way I will test them and see whether they will follow my instructions. (Exodus 16:4 NIV)**

In this way, I will test them and see if they will follow my instructions! Say out loud, "It's a test!" What kind of test? A test to see if you will follow his instructions! A test of your obedience! God gives us instructions, rules, and laws to follow in order to test and bless! Say, "Test and bless!" In this passage we are able to see specific instructions given to Moses to give to the children of Israel.

Continuing…

> **Then the LORD said to Moses, "I will rain down bread from heaven for you. The people are to go out each day and gather enough for that day. In this way I will test them and see whether they will follow my instructions. On the sixth day they are to prepare what they bring in, and that is to be twice as much as they gather on the other days." (Exodus 16:4–5 NIV)**

Let's skip to verses 11–15.

> **The LORD said to Moses, "I have heard the grumbling of the Israelites. Tell them, 'At twilight you will eat meat, and in the morning you will be filled with bread. Then you will know that I am the LORD your God.'" That evening quail came and covered the camp, and in the morning there was a layer of dew around**

> the camp. When the dew was gone, thin flakes like frost on the ground appeared on the desert floor. When the Israelites saw it, they said to each other, "What is it?" For they did not know what it was. Moses said to them, "It is the bread the LORD has given you to eat.

I want you to see where the word *manna* comes from, so I'm going to switch and read verse 15 from the King James Version.

> And when the children of Israel saw it, they said one to another, It is manna: for they wist not what it was. And Moses said unto them, This is the bread which the LORD hath given you to eat.

Back to verse 16 from the NIV:

> This is what the LORD has commanded: "Everyone is to gather as much as they need. Take an omer for each person you have in your tent." The Israelites did as they were told; some gathered much, some little. And when they measured it by the omer.

(OMER IS A MEASUREMENT OF ABOUT THREE POUNDS).

> The one who gathered much did not have too much, and the one who gathered little did not have too little. Everyone had gathered just as much as they needed. Then Moses said to them, "No one is to keep any of it until morning." However, some of them paid no attention to Moses; they kept part of it until morning, but it was full of maggots and began to smell. So Moses was angry with them.

Again, from the Word of God, we can clearly see that there is a blessing in obedience and a curse in disobedience! Say that out loud to yourself say, "It's a blessing in obedience!" This is also a great example and word on tithing! You can give the 10 percent and trust God's promise to bless the 90, or you can hold on to the 10 and lose it all! God's promise is this:

> **And I will rebuke the devourer for your sakes, and he shall not destroy the fruits of your ground; neither shall your vine cast her fruit before the time in the field, saith the LORD of hosts. (Malachi 3:11 KJV)**

Back to where we left off.

> **Each morning everyone gathered as much as they needed, and when the sun grew hot, it melted away. On the sixth day, they gathered twice as much—two omers for each person— and the leaders of the community came and reported this to Moses. He said to them, "This is what the LORD commanded: 'Tomorrow is to be a day of sabbath rest, a holy sabbath to the LORD. So bake what you want to bake and boil what you want to boil. Save whatever is left and keep it until morning.'" So they saved it until morning, as Moses commanded, and it did not stink or get maggots in it. (Exodus 16:21 NIV)**

I feel like right here is a great time to remind you that HE'S A KEEPER! When you obey his will and his word, he will keep you!

> **"Eat it today," Moses said, "because today is a sabbath to the LORD. You will not find any of it on the ground today. Six days**

> **you are to gather it, but on the seventh day, the Sabbath, there will not be any." Nevertheless, some of the people went out on the seventh day to gather it, but they found none. (Exodus 16:25 NIV)**

SMH, there your cousins, your kinfolk go again! And some of us are still doing the same! You're doing exactly what God told you not to do! It's because of this that you continue to find nothing!

> **Then the LORD said to Moses, "How long will you refuse to keep my commands and my instructions? Bear in mind that the LORD has given you the Sabbath; that is why on the sixth day he gives you bread for two days. Everyone is to stay where they are on the seventh day; no one is to go out." So the people rested on the seventh day. (Exodus 16:28 NIV)**

Again, in verse 31 we see the word *manna*:

> **The people of Israel called the bread manna. It was white like coriander seed and tasted like wafers made with honey.**

Let's jump to verse 35.

> **The Israelites ate manna forty years, until they came to a land that was settled; they ate manna until they reached the border of Canaan.**

Remember this, what God uses to fill you now is for now! It is for the season that you're in! Don't ever be misled into thinking that this is all that God has and that it's forever! God has more!

The book of Exodus states that the Israelites consumed the manna for forty years until the manna ceased to appear once they reached a settled land in the borders of Canaan. But again, while they were in the wilderness for forty years, God still supplied their needs! Just as he is doing for many of us still stuck and wandering in your wilderness today, many are still living, still surviving in the wilderness off God's grace and mercy! God has delivered you, he's brought you out, yet you continue to look back. You still want to go back! You're still complaining and murmuring against both God and others! You're still blaming others, "My life is messed up because of you!" "My life is the way that it is because of my mama and daddy!" In reality, you don't deserve even what you have now! Why? Because of your disobedience! Because you haven't obeyed! You haven't listened to God! Yet he's still blessing you! He's still keeping you! You're surviving off his grace and mercy! Just like the children of Israel who wandered in the wilderness until they died having never reached the promise land! Never realizing that God has more! He has more! In his plans for your life there's more! I'm purposely stressing this because I want to make sure that it sinks in! There's more he has prepared or you! There's a promise land waiting for you! A land flowing with milk and honey! Don't stop! Keep going! You're still in the wilderness forgetting that your destiny awaits! There's more than manna! The manna was good for its time and season, but God has more! How do you know, Pastor? I'll tell you how I know, his word says so!

But as it is written, Eye hath not seen, nor ear heard, neither have entered into the heart of man, the things which God hath prepared for them that love him. (1 Corinthians 2:9 KJV)

The manna was good! The manna served a critical purpose in the lives of the children of Israel. There was a message in the manna! God sent the manna to encourage the Israelites! He sent the manna to show them that he was with them and that it was him who brought them out! But there's much more than the manna! I don't know too many people that go to the buffet like Golden Coral or Old Country, don't too many folks go there just to eat salad! I mean, yeah, you might get a salad but it's so much more to indulge in! The manna was good! The manna was in fact a miracle! But today I encourage you, don't stop at the manna! Everything that God has done for you, whatever God has brought you through, you ought to thank him! You ought to praise him! But don't deny him! Don't limit God! Don't ever put God in a box! He's God all alone!

> **"For my thoughts are not your thoughts, neither are your ways my ways," declares the LORD. "As the heavens are higher than the earth, so are my ways higher than your ways and my thoughts than your thoughts." (Isaiah 55:8–9 NIV)**

How far can you see! In Genesis chapter 13, God told Abram,

> **The LORD said to Abram after Lot had parted from him, "Look around from where you are, to the north and south, to the east and west. All the land that you see I will give to you and your offspring forever. I will make your offspring like the dust of the earth, so that if anyone could count the dust, then your offspring could be counted. Go, walk through the length and breadth of the land, for I am giving it to you." (Genesis 13:14–17 NIV)**

Activate your faith!

> **Truly I tell you, if you have faith as small as a mustard seed, you can say to this mountain, 'Move from here to there,' and it will move. Nothing will be impossible for you. (Matthew 17:20 NIV)**

There's a message in the manna! The message is a reminder of the promises of God. God's promise to his children. His promise that he will never leave nor forsake you. His promise to supply all our needs according to his riches in glory. His promise that no weapon formed against you shall prosper and that greater is he that is in you than he that is in the world. And his promise in the Gospel of John 15, which reads:

> **If you remain in me and my words remain in you, ask whatever you wish, and it will be done for you. This is to my Father's glory, that you bear much fruit, showing yourselves to be my disciples. "As the Father has loved me, so have I loved you. Now remain in my love. If you keep my commands, you will remain in my love, just as I have kept my Father's commands and remain in his love. I have told you this so that my joy may be in you and that your joy may be complete. (John 15:7–11 NIV)**

Say this prayer:

> *Thank you, Lord! Thank you for loving me FIRST! Thank you for forgiveness! Thank you for your grace and mercy! Thank you for saving me! Thank you for redeeming me! Thank you for blessing me! Thank you for calling me! Thank you for sanctifying me! Thank you for your plans for my life! Thank you for manna! Thank you for giving me each day my daily bread! Thank you for supplying me each day with whatever it is that I need! Forgive me, Lord, for any time that I have not recognized your blessings or missed your calling! I pray, Lord, that as you continue to supply my every need I ask that you bless me, Lord, with eyes to*

see and ears to hear you! Bless me, Lord, with knowledge, wisdom, and understanding as to your will. Bless me not to become so caught up in the manna that you supply that I miss your message, purpose, or meaning in supplying the manna. Bless me to not miss your movement! Bless me to recognize your voice as you lead and guide me along your will, path, and plans for my life. Bless me to obey your word and bless me to glorify you by being a blessing to others! In Jesus's name, I pray, amen!

9

It Ain't Even Worth It

Are you feeling tired and stressed out from dealing with the same routine, responsibilities, and rigmarole of life? Have you allowed the enemy to steal your joy by focusing on daily tasks, activities, issues, and even people that you have allowed to become a major consumption of your life? This is a word that you need to read today! God led me to write this sermon just to let you know that IT AIN'T EVEN WORTH IT!

As Jesus and the disciples continued on their way to Jerusalem, they came to a certain village where a woman named Martha welcomed him into her home. Her sister, Mary, sat at the Lord's feet, listening to what he taught. But Martha was distracted by the big dinner she was preparing. She came to Jesus and said, "Lord, doesn't it seem unfair to you that my sister just sits here while I do all the work? Tell her to come and help me." But the Lord said to her, "My dear Martha, you are worried and upset over all these details! There is only one thing worth being concerned about. Mary has discovered it, and it will not be taken away from her." (Luke 10:38–42 NLT)

As I wrote in the introduction, I want to bless you on today by briefly writing to you from the sermon title "IT AIN'T EVEN WORTH IT!" Help me get that in your spirit on today by saying that out loud to yourself say, "[YOUR NAME], IT AIN'T EVEN WORTH IT!" I think you need to declare that one more time say it out loud again, "[YOUR NAME], IT AIN'T EVEN WORTH IT!" I can sense that you're probably wondering, "Well, what are you talking about, Pastor?" So now that we've spoken this declaration into the atmosphere, let me tell you what I'm talking about—the gas bill, light bill, phone bill, Comcast, Dish network, Direct TV, or whoever you got! Your car note, your rent, or mortgage payment, any other bills, your credit report, how much money you got left in the bank, how you gon' pay for your prescription, whatever it is that's got you distracted or worried on today! Your career or job, whether you are going to find a job, when and how are you ever going to make it big? If I haven't got to you yet, just hold on, I have to be close to getting in your business. Let me see, your children, your spouse, your man, or woman. When are you going to find you a good man or woman? Your trifling baby mama or baby daddy. In the words of Usher, "Your OH, your OH, your BOO!" Whether this person cheating on you, whether they gon' leave you, or why you can't get them to leave you!? Decisions you've made and what you gon' do now? That lump you found. That boil under your arm. That child support payment. Why so and so don't like you? Why folks keep talking about you? Why can't you just be happy? Why this, why that? Whatever it is that has your focus and attention! Whatever it is that's got you distracted! Whatever it is that's worrying you! I wrote this to let you know and you ought to open your mouth one last time and declare it to yourself right now say, "Today is the last day I'm worrying with this 'cause IT AIN'T EVEN WORTH IT!" Now if you believe it and receive it, give the Lord a hand clap of praise!

The passage that we just read from Luke 10:38–42 is a story that we can learn a valuable lesson from. It's a story about two sisters named Martha and Mary. The passage we just read is not only from the Word of God, but the scripture also contains a rhema or logos word, *rhema* being a Greek word meaning a direct spoken word or utterance from Christ. A rhema word is a word that is for the building up of the body of Christ. It is my prayer that somebody reading this is reading with a hunger, and when I say hunger, I'm talking about a yearning for some good spiritual or "soul" food that might nourish and strengthen your entire life both in your physical as well as your spiritual being. A rhema word! I'm excited for anyone reading this because this rhema word that the Lord has for me to share with you will be a blessing unto you that will lift your burdens and set you on the right path if you can get this in your spirit today.

So again, in the passage we just read, we see a story about two sisters, Martha and Mary. Allow me to give you just a little history in case you don't know but Martha and Mary; Martha being the older sister. They were the sisters of Lazarus whom we can recall Lazarus being the one who Jesus raised from the dead. This happened after this story we're reading about today, but as Jesus would travel and pass through their village, he would stay with them and in doing so he developed a relationship with them. In the story we just read, Jesus is going about and through the villages healing, answering questions, and teaching people. Luke 10:38 says that it came to pass that as they went and were on their way to Jerusalem, they entered a certain village where a woman named Martha welcomed him into her home.

Nothing wrong with that right? I'm sure we've all welcomed someone into our homes before, and I mean this wasn't just somebody this was Jesus! I mean some of y'all reading this ain't never had Jesus in y'all house (LOL)! But you know how it is when you are inviting someone important over. Maybe you're having family or guest from out of town. Maybe you invited your pastor over. But you want to make sure that everything is perfect.

So, Martha after she invites Jesus to her home, I'm sure she made sure he was comfortable and then she went off to the kitchen to start cooking. She probably had some chicken and dressing in the oven, macaroni and cheese, some greens on the stove. Come on, use your imagination with me I'm trying to paint a picture for you! But Martha was busy! She was busy trying to prepare this big meal for Jesus! Again, nothing wrong with that! Now her sister Mary, on the other hand, is believed to be the younger sister. Some of you women reading this may have sisters, and we all know or have heard about sister or sibling rivalries. We should be able to relate to that. But Mary was the younger sister, and the Bible says that while Martha was in the kitchen, cumbered or distracted as my Bible says. Sweating! You know how hot it gets in the kitchen with that oven going. They ain't have no AC back then, so she was probably in there sweating! She was focused, consumed with preparing this big meal. While Mary, the passage says, sat at the Lord's feet. Mary was in there with the men, sitting back, kicking it. Just chilling! Mary wasn't focused on nothing except for listening to what Jesus taught!

Okay, let's go back to Martha, big sis, in the kitchen getting it in! Putting her foot all in them greens! Okay, back to Mary, sitting at the feet of Jesus. I'm sure you can see where this is going. Martha got hot! I'm sure you can relate, Martha got upset! I can just imagine what she was saying to herself! "You know what, I'm tired of this mess! This lazy so and so! She ain't good for nothing!" Martha probably had her hand on her hip, rolling her head. Martha said, "I'm in here cooking all this food, greens and manna! (They probably ain't call it corn bread back then) LOL. (You gon' eat your manna?) Lol! Martha had had enough! She couldn't take it no more. She had to say something! Now, on the low we can see that Martha was also kind of hot with Jesus as well. You know back then it wasn't customary for women to be with the men while they were talking, yet Mary was in there and Jesus hadn't said anything about it. So Martha asks Jesus, "Lord, what kind of mess is this? (I'm paraphrasing of course. This the hip-hop or urban version! The Smith dialect!) But Martha said, "What kind of mess is this? I'm in here making chicken and dressing, macaroni and cheese, greens, corn bread, sweet tea! And this trifling thang ain't did a thing!" Martha said, "Does this seem fair that I do all the work while my sister just sits here?" Martha said, "Tell her to get her but up and come help!" Look, you know she was hot if she was telling Jesus what to do! Don't be too quick to judge her now, 'cause some of us we done told God what he needs to do to more than few times! (I'll put an exclamation point right there.) "God, if you'll just do this and this." Oh, you gon' sit there and act like you ain't never done that before? Tell the truth and shame the devil!

I want to make sure that we understand this about Martha, it's not Martha's service that's wrong. No, it's not her service that's wrong. It's her attitude in service. Yes, it's her attitude in service! Somebody had to serve Jesus. Somebody today still has to serve Jesus! Just like somebody has to serve at your church. But her attitude, my dear Martha! I'm sure you probably know a few Marthas! Especially if you go to church, I'm sure you can testify that it's still a whole lot of Marthas in there! Her attitude in serving was wrong! Say that out loud, say, "It's your attitude!" I've seen it too many times. Sure, we appreciate you and all you do for us. You always here on time. You always doing something to help out. You always look so nice! You have a serving ministry, all you need now is a servant's heart! It wasn't Martha's service, it was Martha's attitude! I spoke awhile back about people that do stuff for you and never let you forget it! They enslave you and some people want you indebted to them for life! Then you got other people that do stuff just so they can be seen! "Look what I did!" "Ain't I a blessing?" No! You really have to be careful about some folks that try to help you 'cause help from the wrong person can turn out to be a curse! It reminds me of this short story I once read titled "**The Non-Conforming Sparrow.**"

THE NON-CONFORMING SPARROW

Once upon a time, there was a non-conforming sparrow who decided not to fly south for the winter. However, soon the weather turned so cold that he reluctantly started to fly south. In a short time, ice began to form on his wings and he fell to earth in a barnyard. Almost frozen, a cow passed by and crapped on the little sparrow. The sparrow thought it can't get much worse than this, this has to be the end. But the manure warmed the sparrow up and defrosted his wings. Warm and happy, able to breathe, the sparrow started to sing. Just then, a large cat came by and hearing the chirping, investigated the sounds. The cat cleared away the manure, found the chirping bird and ate him.

Morals to the story:

- **Everyone who craps on you is not necessarily your enemy.**
- **Everyone who gets you out of some crap is not necessarily your friend.**
- **And if you're warm and happy in a pile of crap, keep your mouth shut!**

So again, you need to be careful about some folks that try and who you allow to help you!

So Martha's attitude was wrong. Let's talk about what was wrong with Martha's attitude. First thing I want to point out is that I don't believe Martha was jealous. No, she wasn't jealous that Mary was spending time with Jesus, she was angry that Mary wasn't helping her. See, it would have been one thing if she was envious because she wanted to be in there listening and sitting at the feet of Jesus too, but Martha was distracted. Her focus was off; she thought that working in the kitchen was the better thing to do, and not only for her, but for Mary as well. You know anybody like that? You know anybody that thinks they know and are always trying to tell you what you ought to be doing, somebody that's always trying to tell you what's best for you, but they can't even get they own life in order? Martha, she didn't have that longing or desire to do nothing else but sit at Jesus feet and listen to him teach. Her focus, in her mind, she thought that she was doing the better thing in focusing on preparing this huge meal! And a lot of us are just like that! A lot of folks don't know they messed up! A lot of us really believe that we are on the right path, doing the right things! Folks believe that it's their job to worry about and make sure everybody else is doing what they are supposed to be doing, even though they are not! You believe it's your job to watch over the church and make sure the right people are in the right position even though God didn't call you to be a pastor! You believe it's your job to make sure that nothing fishy is going on with the finances in the church even though you are not truly tithing yourself! Yeah, I know somebody reading this might not like me no more, but that's okay, Jesus loves me and ain't nothing you can do about it!

Let's look at Luke 10:41. In verse 41, Jesus responds to Martha. Jesus speaks to Martha, a rhema word! And this rhema word Jesus is still speaking to us today! Get this! This right here is going to bless you if you can get it! Luke 10:41–42 says:

> **But the Lord said to her, "My dear Martha, you are worried and upset over all these details! There is only one thing worth being concerned about. Mary has discovered it, and it will not be taken away from her." (Luke 10:41–42 NLT)**

Say out loud, "There is only one thing!" You are worried and upset over all these details! The King James says, **"Thou art careful and troubled about many things"** (Luke 10:41). I preached a sermon awhile back about getting your mind right and setting your mind on high or heavenly and not low or earthly thoughts. Your bills, your job, your children, what the doctor said, all those things I opened with! People and what folks think or have to say about you! Thou are careful and troubled about many things! You are worried and upset over all these details. And most of the time you're worrying about stuff that God has already worked out! Stuff that ain't even going to happen! Remember, there is nothing that has ever happened to us in our entire lives that has ever shocked God! It's FEAR (false evidence appearing real)! Fear is not of God!

> **For God hath not given us the spirit of fear; but of power, and of love, and of a sound mind. (2 Timothy 1:7 KJV)**

The enemy has gotten you off track. He's got a hold of your mind, and he's stolen your vision! He's shifted your focus! Once he shifts your focus, he's able to steal your joy! You become focused on the wrong things, and your emotions now begin to get the best of you. You begin to feel mad, depressed, sad, and confused. Martha is so caught up and worried about this big meal. She's worried about the preparation of food! But I could of swore that my Bible tells me in the Gospel of Mathew that, "Man shall not live off bread alone but on every word that comes from the mouth of God" (Matthew 4:4 NIV)! Martha was so caught up in working, preparing her big meal. She was so distracted with earthly or physical food, that she wasn't focused on the spiritual food and life that was being given right in the next room. Many of us are guilty of the same! Work, work, work, work, work, sounds like a Rihanna song! That's all we know! That's all we do, work, work, work, work, work! This is what our lives have become, working to pay bills! Working to satisfy our earthly needs! But it's important that you know, regardless of how much or how hard you work, your works won't get you there! In preparing this sermon, I did some research and read an article on Bible.org in which I felt the author Bob Deffinbaugh provided some excellent insight on discipleship. He stated that, "True discipleship or the essence of discipleship is not in our works or even our services rendered to Christ but rather it's our finding our sustenance in Christ"! He says, "It's not about being Martha, we need to be more like Mary! True discipleship is not a duty, True discipleship is a devotion and dependence on Christ"![2]

Anything that you do out of duty, your attitude will change after a while! If you don't believe that, just think about your job! Now some of you may love what you do for a living, which is wonderful. But most of us, and I said us because I can definitely remember all of my nine-to-fives. You get up and go to work because you have to! Bills got to be paid. That's right you know the routine, mama

---

[2] Bob Deffinbaugh, "37. When Martha Was Mad at the Master (LUKE 10:38–42)." Bible.org, June 24, 2004, bible.org/seriespage/37-when-martha-was-mad-master-luke-1038-42.

needs a house, baby needs a new pair of shoes! Daddy has got to go to work! Your job becomes a duty! And after a while, duties have a way of becoming a burden. Your attitude, vision, joy, they all begin to change! For my ladies reading this, here's another example. To some of you being a wife becomes a duty. You get tired of cooking, washing, and cleaning up after this lazy (COME ON NOW!) It becomes a duty!

Last but not the least, I wrote about it earlier, but let's talk about church! A lot of folks, specifically "religious folks," come to church out of religion and duty! That's right, I said it! Some folks have just been attending church for so long that it has just become a part of who they are and what they do. It's their religion! They come because they wouldn't know what else to do! They serve and attend out of duty! Duties become burdens! Some of us are so devoted to religion, to duties! Again, you're committed, and we can count on you! But I can definitely tell those that do it out of duty and those that do it out of love and a joyful devotion to Christ! You can tell, amen! One of the main ways you can tell when someone is serving out of duty is this, what's the first thing people do when they get upset in church? They say, "I'm done. I'm not serving anymore!" Why? Because somebody made you mad? Well, if that's the case, who were you serving for in the first place? Are you serving for folks or are you serving for God!? Cause if God called and anointed you for a purpose, and the first, third, or even thirtieth time for that matter, that somebody make you mad or says something that you don't like and you talking about quitting, then who are you really quitting on? Come on now! I have never heard a hater say that they done hating! I have never heard Satan say, "You know what, I'm done trying to steal, kill, and destroy so and so!" They might switch to somebody else for a while but best believe they'll be back! So how is it that we, servants of the highest God, are always the ones that feel like we can quit?

Jesus Christ was teaching a lesson to Martha and the lesson was that of the life he lived. The first lesson he was teaching was a lesson on prioritizing! Jesus prioritized! Everything about Jesus life and ministry was not focused on his will or his agenda, but his father's will! Jesus knew that his time was short, and he must be about his father's business. When the disciples asked Jesus what does a man need to do to get into heaven? Jesus replied, "Love the Lord your God with all your heart, and with all your soul, and with all your strength and mind. And you must love your neighbor as much as you love yourself." That's prioritizing!

In the Gospel of Mathew 6:33, Jesus says:

But seek ye first the kingdom of God, and his righteousness; and all these things shall be added unto you. (Matthew 6:33 KJV)

Again, that's prioritizing. We all must learn to prioritize our lives. Martha, like some of us today, was a busybody. She had a serving ministry but not a servant's heart. She had gotten distracted in the same way that Satan is aiming to distract us today. Our actions won't always be so blatant to the point that we recognize we have strayed from God's path and plans for our life. But the longer that the enemy can keep you distracted and from walking in your purpose is a victory for him. In the Gospel of Luke 9:62, Jeus tells his disciples about distractions:

But Jesus told him, "Anyone who lets himself be distracted from the work I plan for him is not fit for the Kingdom of God." (Luke 9:62 TLB)

Jesus was teaching Martha a lesson about prioritizing. Jesus prioritized. Jesus never allowed the enemy to distract him. Jesus knew that his time was short. Why is it that we think we still have so much time?

Jesus was also teaching another lesson to Martha and the lesson again was that of the life he lived! It was a lesson of life and purpose. In Luke 10:42, Jesus tells Martha:

There is only one thing worth being concerned about. Mary has discovered it, and it

will not be taken away from her. (Luke 10:42 NLT)

When you learn who you are and discover your purpose, you will no longer allow yourself to be sidetracked by Satan or by all these other details that truly don't matter! You won't stray from that path and purpose that God has called you to. You will learn the lesson that Jesus was teaching in verse 42. You will discover that "there is only one thing worth being concerned about!" You will learn like the song Earth Wind and Fire sings, to "Keep Your Head to the Sky!" You'll learn what David sang in the book of Psalms to lift up your eyes and look to the hills from which cometh your help (Psalm 121:1). David said, **"Yea though I walk through the valley of the shadow of death, I will fear no evil: for thou art with me; Thy rod and thy staff they comfort me"** (Psalm 23:4 KJV). Sure, you might have haters all around you hating you, but you can't focus on that. That's what haters do! In fact, if you don't have any haters, then might I suggest that you must not be doing something right then! Or if you ain't got no haters, then it might be that you the hater! Why focus on your haters? You already know the enemy is plotting on you! You already know that he wants to steal, kill, and destroy you! That's his purpose! So since you already know that, then why would you focus on that? Read the scriptures, David said, **"Thou prepare a table before me in the presence of mine enemies"** (Psalm 23:5)! You better focus on the table that's been prepared for you! You better focus on getting to your table and getting all that God said that you could have!

You have to learn how to eat right in your enemy's face! I'm serious! Haters, Satan, your enemies, they're not going nowhere! You ever been somewhere, and you are having a good time then somebody walks in that you might not like or care for, for whatever reason, and it just changes your whole attitude? They walk in and you don't even want to be there anymore, you are ready to go! Well, right there Satan done got the best of you! Right there Satan threw your focus all the way off and made you forget that quick who you are! You are the salt of the earth! You are the light of the world! You are an ambassador for the kingdom of God! Greater is he that is in you than he that is in the world! What are you letting your spirit get infected for? What are you leaving the party for? If anything, they ought to be the ones leaving when you walk in! Say, amen! Let's close this out.

IT AIN'T WORTH IT! Say out loud, "IT AIN'T WORTH IT!" All these things, this stuff, this mess that Satan uses to distract and consume us! To steal our joy and infect us with sickness in both our bodies and spirit! To have us live a life of fear rather than a life of abundance! An anointed life! A life of true discipleship and true service to God. We live our lives consumed with things of this world when the Bible clearly tells us to be in this world but not of this world. And I can still hear somebody in my spirit. I hear you saying, "Well, Pastor, it all sounds good, but how can I not be worried about my lights about to get cut off, or my car about to get repossessed." "How can I not be worried about my kids?" "How can I not worry about these things?" "What am I supposed to do, Pastor?" I'll tell you! How about TRUST GOD! How about have faith in Jesus, in the only begotten son of God! Have faith in the one who loves you and gave himself for you! How about stand on the Word of God! What I'm writing to you and you're reading on today, that it ain't worth it! What I'm telling you not to worry about! This ain't me, this is the Word of God! That rhema word! I could show you all day!

> **Do not be anxious about anything, but in every situation, by prayer and petition, with thanksgiving, present your requests to God. (Philippians 4:6 NIV)**

The New Living Translation reads:

> **Don't worry about anything; instead, pray about everything. Tell God what you need, and thank him for all he has done. (Philippians 4:6–7 NLT)**

As Stevie Wonder sang, "Don't you worry about a thang!"

Or what about the Gospel of Matthew 6:25–34. Jesus says:

> **"Therefore I tell you, do not worry about your life, what you will eat or drink; or about your body, what you will wear. Is not life more than food, and the body more than clothes? Look at the birds of the air; they do not sow or reap or store away in barns, and yet your heavenly Father feeds them. Are you not much more valuable than they? Can any one of you by worrying add a single hour to your life? And why do you worry about clothes? See how the flowers of the field grow. They do not labor or spin. Yet I tell you that not even Solomon in all his splendor was dressed like one of these. If that is how God clothes the grass of the field, which is here today and tomorrow is thrown into the fire, will he not much more clothe you— you of little faith? So do not worry, saying, 'What shall we eat?' or 'What shall we drink?' or 'What shall we wear?' For the pagans run after all these things, and your heavenly Father knows that you need them. But seek first his kingdom and his righteousness, and all these things will be given to you as well. Therefore do not worry about tomorrow, for tomorrow will worry about itself. Each day has enough trouble of its own." (Matthew 6:25–34 NIV)**

Two scriptures I want to elaborate on from that passage and I'm done. First, verse 26 reads:

> **Look at the birds of the air; they do not sow or reap or store away in barns, and yet your heavenly Father feeds them. Are you not much more valuable than they?**

That verse takes me back to the old church. I can remember being a kid and hearing the old church singing "**His Eye Is on the Sparrow.**" The lyrics were:

> Why should I feel discouraged,
> Why should the shadows come,
> Why should my heart feel lonely
> And long for Heav'n and home,
> When Jesus is my portion?
> A constant Friend is He:
> His eye is on the sparrow,
> And I know He watches over me;
> I sing because I'm happy,
> I sing because I'm free,
> His eye is on the sparrow,
> And I know He watches me
> Hallelujah!!

The second verse from that passage that I want to elaborate on is verse 32 which reads:

> **For the pagans run after all these things, and your heavenly Father knows that you need them.**

Verse 32 reiterates and reminds us that HE KNOWS YOUR NEEDS! He knows you need a job! He knows what the doctor said! He knows you're worried about your baby being out in the streets or in jail! Remember, nothing has ever happened in your life that shocked God! So if he knows about it, then it ain't your job to be worrying about it! Matthew 6:33 said:

> **But seek first his kingdom and his righteousness, and all these things will be given to you as well.**

HE WILL PROVIDE YOUR EVERY NEED!

David said it best in Psalm 37:25. He said:

I have been young, and now am old; yet have I not seen the righteous forsaken, nor his seed begging bread. (Psalm 37:25 KJV)

When Satan can steal your joy, he can steal your vision and change your focus. He can then get you to worry, and once you're worried, he can get you to make bad choices or decisions. Ultimately, our decisions impact and affect the direction of our lives! Just look at what's going on in the news with the violence all around the world. All the robberies, and murders, you go in planning to rob a pizzeria and you lose your life or end up in jail for the rest of your life. Most of the bad decisions we make are because we've lost our faith and focus, and we are worrying about the wrong things! We're worrying about the details! Fear sets in and your thought process is that you're hungry and you need to eat but you can't get a job, you got no money, so now you think that you have to rob somebody! It ain't even worth it!

It AIN'T WORTH IT! Whatever it is that's got you worried on today! Whatever it is Martha that you're so busy doing! IT AIN'T WORTH IT! Whatever it is that you spend your time doing, whatever it is that's keeping you from Jesus! And just like Martha, it might not be that whatever it is that you're doing is bad or worldly. Like I said earlier, some of us have a serving ministry, we just need a servant's heart! You're distracted and you're wrapped up in and worried about the wrong things, church folks worried about why so and so over this or that ministry? Why doesn't the pastor sit on the stage? Why doesn't this person do nothing? Look, when you're out of your lane that's when you get stressed! That's when it gets hard! You have been trying to do everything! Trying to figure it all out for yourself! You been chasing everything but God! But you have never stopped and just sat at his feet long enough to hear him! To hear what he's saying! That's why you're tired, that's why you're sweating!

Then Jesus said, "Come to me, all of you who are weary and carry heavy burdens, and I

will give you rest. Take my yoke upon you. Let me teach you, because I am humble and gentle at heart, and you will find rest for your souls. For my yoke is easy to bear, and the burden I give you is light." (Matthew 11:28–30 NLT)

Luke 10:42 Jesus says to Martha:

There is only one thing worth being concerned about. Mary has discovered it, and it will not be taken away from her. (Luke 10:42 NLT)

Mary found her treasure!

Don't store up treasures here on earth, where moths eat them and rust destroys them, and where thieves break in and steal. Store your treasures in heaven, where moths and rust cannot destroy, and thieves do not break in and steal. Wherever your treasure is, there the desires of your heart will also be. (Matthew 6:19–21 NLT)

I can hear that old church singing again!
Hold to his hand God's unchanging hand,
Hold to his hand God's unchanging hand.
Build your hopes on things eternal,
Hold to God's unchanging hand!!!
Say this prayer:

Gracious and Heavenly Father, thank you for wisdom! Thank you for showing me your will, purpose, and plans for my life! Thank you for showing me what's important, Lord! Teach me how to focus on those things that glorify you! Teach me how to walk by faith and not by sight! Hear me when I cast all of my cares upon you knowing that it is you that cares for me! Supply all of me needs according to your riches and glory by Christ Jesus! Care for me as you do the sparrow. Forgive me, Lord, for concerning myself with things of this world. Restore the time, energy, and peace, which I have lost by worrying and chasing things of this world. Lead me, guide me, order my steps for your glory! In Jesus's name, amen.

10

Sowing a Seed in Soil to Succeed (Part 1)

We've all heard the saying, "You reap what you sow." Well, this is actually more than just a saying! Sowing is a biblical principle, foundation, and the blueprint to which all your life's goals, dreams, and desires shall come to pass. Sowing is the works that allows you to obtain the substance of your faith. A wise farmer once said, "If you never plant the seeds today, don't expect to eat a harvest tomorrow." This sermon teaches us the importance and power of a seed and how to sow that seed in the correct soil to ensure you succeed! Enjoy!

The same day went Jesus out of the house, and sat by the sea side. And great multitudes were gathered together unto him, so that he went into a ship, and sat; and the whole multitude stood on the shore. And he spake many things unto them in parables, saying, Behold, a sower went forth to sow; And when he sowed, some seeds fell by the way side, and the fowls came and devoured them up: Some fell upon stony places, where they had not much earth: and forthwith they sprung up, because they

had no deepness of earth: And when the sun was up, they were scorched; and because they had no root, they withered away. And some fell among thorns; and the thorns sprung up, and choked them: But other fell into good ground, and brought forth fruit, some an hundredfold, some sixtyfold, some thirtyfold. Who hath ears to hear, let him hear. (Matthew 13:1–9 KJV)

When Jesus would teach, he would use parables. One of the reasons for this can be found in the Old Testament of the Bible in the Book of Isaiah. In Isaiah 6, you can read of where God's patience had run out with the people of Jerusalem and Judah. Though they had witnessed many miracles of God, they were still unbelievers, just like the Jewish leaders and pharisees in the Gospel of Matthew. Because of this, God spoke a curse through the Prophet Isaiah, which caused their hearts to become hardened, their ears to become dull and God closed their eyes so that they would not see, hear, understand, and turn to God so that he could heal them. This was the curse! And so, when Jesus spoke in parables, such as we just read in our sermon scripture, it was almost like a secret language. Even today only those who are receptive to spiritual truths and principles are permitted to understand the kingdom of heaven. As you will learn, there are some who will read and hear the same message and gospel that you once heard, but they will not receive it! To them, it will simply be a story without meaning! They just won't be able to understand how three are one! They won't be able to understand how the Father, the Son and the Holy Spirit are all one in the same! It just won't make sense because their hearts have been hardened, and their eyes and ears have been closed. It's a blessing in which you ought to take a second and thank God as the prophet Jeremiah said for choosing you! For knowing you even before he formed you in your mother's womb! You ought to thank him for sanctifying you and appointing you to service! You didn't choose God, God chose you! He planted you like a seed in a garden, and he told you to be fruitful and multiply! Say that out loud to yourself say, "Be fruitful and multiply!" That was the commandment! Now this is the question, what kind of fruit are you producing? Yes, what kind of seed are you? What kind of sower are you? What kind of farmer and seeds are you sowing?

Let me define sowing. *Sowing* is the process of planting seeds. You plant a seed so that you reap the harvest. Now we should all know about seeds. A seed is a self-contained unit designed for the reproduction of a species. From the book of Genesis, where we learn about the beginning of creation, you will find a "law of Genesis," which basically explains how everything that God created comes from and reproduces after its own kind. For example, Genesis 1:11–12 reads:

> **And God said, Let the earth bring forth grass, the herb yielding seed, and the fruit tree yielding fruit after his kind, whose seed is in itself, upon the earth: and it was so. And the earth brought forth grass, and herb yielding seed after his kind, and the tree yielding fruit, whose seed was in itself, after his kind: and God saw that it was good. (Genesis 1:11–12 KJV)**

> **And God created great whales, and every living creature that moveth, which the waters brought forth abundantly, after their kind, and every winged fowl after his kind: and God saw that it was good. And God blessed them, saying, Be fruitful, and multiply, and fill the waters in the seas, and let fowl multiply in the earth. (Genesis 1:21–22 KJV)**

> **And God said, Let the earth bring forth the living creature after his kind, cattle, and creeping thing, and beast of the earth after his kind: and it was so. And God made the beast of the earth after his kind, and cattle after their kind, and every thing that creepeth upon the**

> **earth after his kind: and God saw that it was good. And God said, Let us make man in our image, after our likeness: and let them have dominion over the fish of the sea, and over the fowl of the air, and over the cattle, and over all the earth, and over every creeping thing that creepeth upon the earth. (Genesis 1:24–26 KJV)**

This pretty much kills the evolution theory I'd say! Those that embrace the theory of evolution represent those that we spoke of who have been cursed and deny the power and design of God. Everything that God created is self-sustaining and self-perpetuating. If you look at a seed, what we discover is that an apple tree produces apples that contain seeds. These apple seeds produce other trees to come into existence, which produce more apples and more seeds. This represents a self-perpetuating system of apple reproduction. No matter how many apples come from the seeds produced, they all originated from the one. Just to reiterate the "law of Genesis" explains how everything will reproduce after its own kind. In other words, a cat doesn't come from a dog. A watermelon doesn't come from an orange. And we didn't come from the apes! Everything that God created comes from and reproduces after its own kind. In the beginning, God created and planted Adam. Adam was the first human seed, and so we all then come from Adam. Jesus was the first spiritual seed and so to have eternal life, we all must be born again in the spirit. So if Adam was the first human seed, then God also planted you as a seed. Seeds bear fruit. Seeds reproduce. As a seed, God expects you to be fruitful and multiply.

The seed and the study of the seed is quite amazing! Although we won't go as deep into it as we could in this sermon, it is a subject in which you could spend weeks studying. I plan to come back and teach a series on the power of a seed but for the purpose of this sermon I'll just do a brief overview of the seed in relation to our lesson today. Basically, the law of genesis along with the reproduction and populating of the Earth was all accomplished by God through seeds.

As we briefly looked at in the book of Genesis chapter 1, in the beginning when God began creating the heavens and the earth, we know that on the first day he created light. He divided the light from the darkness calling the light daytime and the darkness nighttime. On the second day, he separated the sky above and the oceans below. On the third day, he gathered the water into oceans so that dry land would emerge, and he said let the earth burst forth with every sort of grass and seed-bearing plant, and fruit trees with seeds inside the fruit, so that these seeds will produce the kinds of plants and fruits they came from. On the fourth day, he created the sun, moon, stars, and seasons. On the fifth day, he created great sea animals and every sort of fish and bird and told them to multiply and stock the oceans and fill the earth. And on the sixth day, he created every kind of animal, cattle, reptiles, and wildlife of every kind. And then God created man. God created man in his image and made him master over all. God gave man dominion over all and over the seeds.

Genesis chapter 2 continues with detailing God's creation and tell us that there was a river that ran through the garden, which watered the plants and trees. The Lord God placed man in the garden to tend and care for it telling him that he could eat freely from every tree in the garden except from the tree of knowledge of good and evil. He warned Adam that if they ate from that tree, then they would surely die. Now we all know the story of how Satan entered the garden and deceived Eve and she ate of the fruit. She also took the fruit to Adam, and he ate it as well. Well, once Adam did this, God's plan for man changed! Adam, the first human seed, ate of the fruit and because he ate of the fruit curses came to all humans. Again, seeds reproduce and reproduce of their own kind. Through this, we can see the power of a seed! As the saying goes, one apple can spoil the whole bunch! Consequently, it's through the first natural or human seed Adam that we all share the same fate. The curse passed down to us all! This explanation can also be tied to generational curses, which I will also write about at some point. Because Adam disobeyed, because he wasn't obedient, sin did abound. Because of sin, we were cursed with death and other curses. God cursed the soil and man to struggle to make a living from it. There was also now separation in which before sin we know that God did dwell with Adam and Eve. The plan changed from at first when God had made it to where man was blessed with abundance without having to work for it, **no sweat**, to where now God said that you will sweat to master the soil and make a living from it until your dying day. God expelled man from the Garden and sent him to farm the ground from which he came. It is through one seed that we all share the same fate.

Let's look at the power of a seed in its ability to multiply. Fruit both comes from seeds as well as has the seeds necessary to produce more fruit. This is the natural law of multiplication. Most seeds that you plant in the ground always produce multiple or multiplied new seeds. For example, if you plant a seed of corn in the ground, it will grow a new plant that can have anywhere from one to eight new ears of corn on it. Each of those ears of corn can contain anywhere from two hundred to four hundred new seeds! So doing the math on that, we can say one kernel of corn seed is potentially multiplied into as many as $(8 \times 400 = 3,200)$ new seeds. Now, if you take these 3,200 new seeds and plant them, potentially you get $3,200 \times 3,200$ which equals 10,240,000 (ten million, two hundred and forty thousand) new seeds! This is more than just multiplied growth. It is now becoming exponential growth! This represents the power of a single seed! It only takes one seed to have exponential, explosive growth. From two people, we now today have a world population of over seven billion! This also reveals to us our power as Christians when two seeds come together. There is miraculous multiplication and power to the extent where the Bible says that one of us (one seed), can send one thousand demons to flight, but two of us (two seeds), can send ten thousand demons to flight! That's miraculous multiplication! Do I have any seeds reading this who are ready to "seed up" with me? Shout, "Seed up!" This is just an overview of a seed and the power of a seed. Let's move on.

As I said earlier, God knew us before we were in our mother's womb. He planted us and told us to be fruitful and multiply. Which means that we are expected to bear fruit! "How do we bear fruit Pastor H?" I'm glad you asked! We bear fruit by the same process in which we were created. We bear fruit by sowing. If you don't sow any seeds, then you won't produce any harvest. As the word says, we reap what we sow! Let's put some Bible on this and recall what the Word of God says and what happens if you don't produce any fruit. Do you recall the fig tree from the Gospel of Mark chapter 11? Mark chapter 11 tells us a story of where Jesus was hungry and so he went to the fig tree but found that it had no fruit, and so he cursed the fig tree saying it will never bear fruit again and the tree withered away. Have you ever seen a person that's just withering away? I mean they just look like zombies or like a skeleton wearing clothes. That's a person that's not producing any fruit. The gospels say: For to him who has will more be given and he will have more abundance but from him who has not, even the little he has will be taken away. We are to be fruitful and multiply! We are to produce a harvest. Read what Jesus says about a tree and its fruit in Matthew 7.

> **"Watch out for false prophets. They come to you in sheep's clothing, but inwardly they are ferocious wolves. By their fruit you will recognize them. Do people pick grapes from thornbushes, or figs from thistles? Likewise, every good tree bears good fruit, but a bad tree bears bad fruit. A good tree cannot bear bad fruit, and a bad tree cannot bear good fruit. Every tree that does not bear good fruit is cut down and thrown into the fire. Thus, by their fruit you will recognize them. (Matthew 7:15–20 NIV)**

Jesus says you can tell a tree by its fruit, by the fruit it produces.

Let's take the natural into the spiritual. The Bible teaches us that there are two types of fruit, the fruit of the spirit and the fruit of the flesh. We've already discussed Adam and the fall of man. Adam sinned, and because of this first sin, sin passed down to us all. For through flesh, we were born in sin and sharpened in iniquity. Which is why we need to be born again in the spirit. We all have a sinful nature. That simply means that it's our nature to sin! Nobody had to teach you how to sin, it came naturally! **You're a natural!** Galatians 5 tells us to walk in the spirit, obey the Holy Spirit's instructions so that we won't always be fulfilling the lust of our flesh, doing the wrong things that we naturally love to do. Now, when we hear the word *lust*, we tend to think sexual. But lust can be a number of things. But our spirit and our flesh are constantly at war, fighting against each other for control over us. This is an everyday struggle. Think about it like the cartoons or shows that we see on television where they show a character with an angel over one shoulder and a devil over the other. When we follow our sinful nature, the fruit of the flesh, then our lives produce these acts: sexual immorality, impure thoughts, eagerness for lustful pleasure, idolatry and witchcraft; hatred, discord always fighting, jealousy, fits of rage, anger, selfish ambition, always trying to do and get what's best only for you, complaints and criticisms, dissensions, factions, which is groups or clicks and the feeling that everyone else is wrong except those in your own little group. It also says that there will be envy; drunkenness, murder, wild parties, and the like. Have you ever seen these fruits? Sure you have! We all know exactly where to find some of these trees. They are everywhere, aren't they? Some as close as in our own yards and at our own homes! Paul warns us that those who live like this will not inherit the kingdom of God. But when we allow the Holy Spirit to control our lives, the Holy Spirit produces different fruits in us. The fruits of the spirit produce first and foremost love, which is the greatest fruit and spirit of all. The other fruits of the spirit are joy, peace, patience, long-suffering, kindness, goodness, faithfulness, gentleness, and self-control. Oh, how important that last one is. Have you ever been outside of yourself and just out of control! Then you know! With these fruits, or the fruit of the spirit, there is no conflict with Christ. Those of us who belong to Christ, those of us living by the power of the Holy Spirit should bear this fruit.

In our sermon scripture for today from Matthew 13, as you read through the rest of the parable, you'll discover God's goal for giving us His seed. God is looking for a people to produce spiritual fruit. The majority of the parable is a lesson of why people either produce this fruit (the fruit of the spirit) or why they are unable to produce this fruit. If you know anything about farming, you know that the soil is not the master of the seed, but the seed is the master of the soil. Whatever is planted into the soil is that which is harvested. So again, YOU REAP WHAT YOU SOW. Now fruit doesn't just grow. Seeds don't just grow on their own. There is a process to reproduction. Certain things must happen, certain environments must exist. You must sow a seed. You have to plant a seed and that seed needs to have the right elements and conditions to grow. I went over how God created the heavens and the earth with seeds and how he created the environment necessary for the seeds to grow. seeds won't just grow on their own. They need water and sunlight. So it needs the son (sun)! I hope somebody is getting this! It needs soil and not just any soil but preferably good soil. As the scriptures and parable, we read for our sermon today shows us, you can sow your seed in many types of soil. Just as there are good and bad seeds, there is good and bad soil.

We need to learn from the parable today. We need to have ears that hear so that we will know how to sow our seed in soil to succeed! Matthew 13:3–9 tells us the different types of soil that the sower planted his seed, it reads:

> **And he spake many things unto them in parables, saying, Behold, a sower went out to sow. And as he sowed, some *seed* fell by the wayside; and the birds came and devoured them. Some fell on stony places, where they did not have much earth; and they immediately sprang up because they had no depth of earth. But when the sun was up they were scorched, and because they had no root they withered away. And some fell among thorns, and the thorns sprang up and choked them. But others fell on good ground and yielded a crop: some a hundredfold, some sixty, some thirty. He who has ears to hear, let him hear. (Matthew 13: 3–9 KJV)**

You are a seed planted by God to produce, to be fruitful and multiply. The way that we produce is by reproduction by sowing. By planting seeds. We know the type of fruit that we are to produce, and we know the seeds necessary. We know the seeds we need to plant. And we know that we will reap what we sow. If you sow or if you plant hate, then you can expect to reap hatred. If your thoughts aren't pure, then your actions won't be pure, for you will ultimately go where you are thinking! If you're angry or bitter, if you love to fight, if you're selfish, jealous, and can't take criticism; if no one can tell you anything because you are always right and everybody else is wrong outside of you and your click; if all you do is drink and get high, party like a rock star; if these are the seeds that you sow, then you will reproduce seeds that do the same! And you will reap all that comes along with what you've sown. Translation, hating men marry hating women that have hating babies, and they become all in the hating family!

The parable is now switching from the sower and the seed to telling us the different types of soil upon which the seeds fell. **SOME SEEDS FELL BY THE WAYSIDE.** Jesus explains the parable by saying that the seed that fell by the wayside represents the heart of a person who hears the Good News about the kingdom and doesn't understand it and so the enemy comes and quickly, easily, snatches away the seed from his heart! At the start of the sermon, we talked about how God has a plan for our lives and how Satan wants to destroy that plan just as he did in the Garden of Eden with Adam and Eve. Now here we see the enemy, whose plan never changes—steal, kill, and destroy. Here we see him in action. In the parable, it says he snatches the seed, the Good News, the Word of God that the person didn't understand, and so it fell by the wayside where the enemy quickly snatched it up. The soil which the seed fell on is the wayside. So what is the wayside? The wayside is the side or edge of a road, way, path, or highway. To *fall by the wayside* means to fail to continue or to give up. To **go by the wayside** is to be set aside or discarded because of other considerations or something more important. Can you recall the story of the young man who wanted to follow Jesus? He heard the Good News and asked Jesus, "Master, what must I do to be saved?" Jesus told him to go and sell all his possessions, and he walked way. He fell, he went by the wayside. We all know people who tell us all the time that they are going to come to church, and they are going to get their life right, but they ain't ready, they are still doing whatever it is they do. And so, they say that they ain't gon' come in the church and play with God like all the rest of them folks that's in church, them hypocrites is playing. "Naw, I ain't gon' do that!" that's what they say, as if what they are doing now is more urgent or more important.

When the seed fell by the wayside, Satan **QUICKLY** snatched it up. Satan knew its worth! That's like if I dropped some money right now you would instantly recognize, "Hey, that's worth something," and pick it up quickly. But as for the young man that went to Jesus and wouldn't sell his riches, and to the person who won't stop whatever it is that they're doing or whatever it is that's more important and has them by the wayside. They don't understand! They don't see the value of the seed! They don't know what you now know today that blessed are your eyes for they see and blessed are your ears for they hear! They don't understand for to him that has more will be given, and he will have great plenty but from him who has not, even the little he has will be taken away. Somebody reading this needs to take just twenty seconds and give God some praise even if it's just for the little that you have! Come on, take twenty more seconds and give him some praise and thanks for allowing you to see what you see and to hear what you hear! Thank him for not letting you fall by the wayside! You need to know that whatever you give to God, God will multiply it and give it back to you! Don't you know that we serve a God that took two fish and five loaves of bread that means he took what wasn't enough, and after he blessed it, it multiplied! He divided it and fed five thousand with leftovers! Look, I ain't gotta go that far back! You can sit there and act like God ain't never did nothing for you, like you've always had it so good. You can act like your bills ain't never been more that your paycheck or more than you got in both your checking and savings account! All some of us got or know is the promise of God! David said:

> **I was young and now I am old, yet I have**
> **never seen the righteous forsaken or their chil-**
> **dren begging bread. (Psalm 37:25 NIV)**

I know what God can do! I know he's able! I'm a living witness! Can't he do it? Wont he do it? Look, if you're reading this and you won't praise him, just know when I wrote this, I went to praising him by myself! He's worthy! Somebody out there reading this knows like me that it's been sometimes in my life where I didn't have nothing but the promises of God! I didn't know how I was going to make it out! But greater is he that is in me than he that is in the world! Somebody reading this you might be going through right now! But forgive us, Lord, for acting like we ain't never seen and heard! This ain't the first time you been down and out. If he brought you out, then won't he most surely do it again! Shout, "There is nothing that's too hard for my God!" Shout, "He's able!"

Sowing a seed in soil that succeeds. God said be fruitful and multiply! You sow so that you can reap a harvest! You will reap what you sow! It's not God's will that you lack for anything! Just like with our kids. Think about how it hurts you to see your kids lack something they need, to go without. And I ain't talking a PS5 or some Jordans, I'm talking about a need as in food or medicine. Think about how bad we feel when we see our children in need, especially when we can't help them! That's not our father's will for our lives!

**"For I know the plans I have for you,"
declares the LORD, "plans to prosper you and
not to harm you, plans to give you hope and a
future." (Jeremiah 29:11 NIV)**

God set his plan of abundance for us in the Garden of Eden. God had a system for blessing us. God said you may eat of all the trees in the garden but from the tree of knowledge of good and evil. God was teaching Adam and Eve about divine portion! God had supplied all their needs! Just like we do with our kids. We get them everything they need and want in a lot of cases, but we tell them, "Okay, that's yours, this is mine!" Don't touch what's mine! That's divine portion. I got my son a cell phone for Christmas one year, a nice one. Now I have an iPhone. I had to explain to him, "Look, that's yours, this is mine!" The system that God has set up to bless us today is tithing. Tithing is not only about money, tithing is about sacrifice. We tithe in our finances as well as in our time! We tithe in our service. We sacrifice in our obedience. God is teaching us. God is testing us. He only asked for a tenth (10 percent). God said if he can't trust us in small things, then he won't be able to trust in in greater things. He won't be able to increase us. God gave it to you, everything you needed! He gave you the job. He gave you the income for the house, car, bills, everything! God said you keep the 90 percent, just give me the 10. The tenth is mine! God doesn't need your money! He's the creator of all things! Again, he doesn't need your money! It's about divine portion! It's a system to bless you. It's like playing catch with God only you throw him the ball, and he throws you back a much bigger ball. It's about love! It's about reaping and reaping what you sow! It's about giving! Giving is love! To worship in giving whether through your church or if you don't have a church home, then in your community, should be one of your favorite parts of service. This is where you have the opportunity to show God how much you love him! This is where you have the opportunity to sow a seed. A seed of obedience. A seed in good soil guaranteed to multiply and produce a great harvest in your life! A seed guaranteed to set you up to succeed! A seed that puts you in position to receive what God has purposed for you. The Lord almighty says:

> **"Bring the whole tithe into the storehouse, that there may be food in my house. Test me in this," says the LORD Almighty, "and see if I will not throw open the floodgates of heaven and pour out so much blessing that there will not be room enough to store it." (Malachi 3:10 NIV)**

The more you love someone the more you will give them! Don't tell me that you love somebody that you won't give anything to! The Bible says that God loves a cheerful giver! So, if you're going to give, give freely! God says give just as freely as it was given unto you. I'm showing you how to sow your seed! This is also important, when you give, make sure that your heart is in the right place. In other words, don't give to get. I'll say it again, don't give to receive. Give out of love! Give because you love God! Don't look at sowing, tithing, or giving with an attitude of I'm going to do it so that I can be blessed. I'm going to do it so that I can get this or that. No, even though you will be blessed, you don't do it for that purpose. This is how you sow your seed. This is how you sow your seed in soil to succeed. We've all sown before. But where were you sowing? I mean come on, some of us have been some straight up "sucka for loves" before. Some of you have given your first and your last, your all, to somebody that YOU KNEW wouldn't give it back! But you know what, you didn't care! You did it because you loved them! Even though you knew that they didn't deserve it!

So many times, we seek God's hand, what he can do for us, but we don't seek his face! Do it because you love him! Do it because he's worthy! Do it because he loves you! The reason God told you to do it is because he loves you! He wants to bless you! He wants to show you more and more! God said if you love me, you'll keep my commandments. Adam and Eve were disobedient. Because of that, curses came. God doesn't curse us. God's will is that we would lack for nothing! We curse ourselves! So we can do like Adam and Eve and be disobedient. We can listen to the serpent or enemy and allow Satan to steal our blessings and change God's plan for our lives. You can keep what belongs to God for whatever reasons the enemy tells you that you should keep it. The enemy will show you your bills and ask you how can you afford to pay this if you give the church that? It's a lie because you're not giving it to the church, you're giving it back to God! Divine portion! Satan will tell you to keep it because you're giving it to a crooked pastor to do God know what with? This is another lie! It's not about the pastor, your obedience and giving is between you and God! As a pastor, I'm going to get my abundance and increase based off the same system that I'm telling you. Satan will tell you all sorts of things to deceive you. To get you to keep what's God's or even to give it unwilling. In which case, you might as well have kept it for yourself because it won't be blessed. God looks at the heart. So keep the tenth and allow Satan to curse the ninety or you can follow the plans that God has for your life! Ten cents on the dollar. Is God not worth a dime? We want increase. We want to be blessed. But can God trust us? Now when you have no or very little income then it's probably easy to give 10 percent. Ten percent of one hundred dollars is only ten dollars. But what happens when God increases you to one thousand dollars a week? That's one hundred dollars. Can God still trust you? Okay, so what if you can see getting to ten thousand dollars, now it's one thousand dollars! Now we're talking about our tithe being rent or a mortgage note. Can he still trust you? I've got news for you, if he can't trust you where you are now, then why would he increase you?

We often sing these songs, and we get caught up in the rhythm or the beat. We be dancing and bopping our heads, which Satan often uses to steal a seed by allowing that seed to fall on some other soil. But in the music, both gospel and secular, we need to listen and understand what we are bopping our heads to. Some of the worldly stuff is just crazy! And we just be dancing away! Even with gospel music, sometimes the beat is so catchy but are you listening? Do you hear what they are saying? A great example is a song by Donald Lawrence, "Let's Get Back to Eden." Do you know this song? Well, did you listen?

> **When God made man, He made a spirit**
> **It was His plan that we live blessed**
> **The tempter came we were distracted**
> **The tempter came and we fell**
> **We were deemed to live a life that's beautiful;**
> **a life that's full; a life that's rich and plentiful**
> **It is my goal to remind you of this principle**
> **You're redeemed; a newborn soul**
> **Let's get back to Eden; live on top of the world**

How are you going to get there? You're not just gon' Holy Ghost–dance back to Eden. Naw, that's not gon' happen!

Mary Mary got a song, "It's the God in Me"! In it, they say, "What is it you think you see when you see me? You don't know how much I prayed, don't know how much I gave, don't know much I changed, I'm just trying to explain." God has a plan for our lives! God has a system for his plan! Sowing a seed into soil to succeed. We sow by being fruitful, by producing fruit and multiplying. God gives the increase. God multiplies what we sow! Be fruitful and multiply! Be fruitful and you will multiply! Sow and you will reap what you sow!

Say this prayer:

> *Gracious and Heavenly Father, thank you for your loving me. Thank you for your plans for my life! Plans to prosper and not to harm me. Plans to give me hope and a future. Thank you for your seed. Your seed that has been planted since you created the heavens and the earth and your seed that has been planted in me today. Bless me to be obedient, Lord. Bless me to be a sower, Lord! Blessed me to sow a seed in soil that succeeds. Don't allow the enemy to steal my seed, Lord. Bless it to fall on good soil. Bless it to multiply and produce a harvest that glorifies you. Bless me to be fruitful and multiply as you have commanded that I might be blessed all the days of my life. That when I meet you I might here you say unto me, "Servant, job well done." In Jesus's name, I pray, amen.*

11

Sowing a Seed in Soil to Succeed (Part 2)

In part 1 of this powerful sermon, we focused on sowing as a biblical principle, foundation, and the blueprint to which all your life's goals, dreams, and desires shall come to pass. We learned that sowing is the works that allows one to obtain the substance of your faith. In part 1, we focused on the power of a seed in God's plan for creation. In part 2 of this series, we will focus on the importance of the soil necessary in order to sow a seed in soil to succeed.

Let's begin this sermon by recapping what we learned in part 1 of "Sowing a Seed in Soil to Succeed." We learned that sowing is the process of planting seeds. You plant a seed so that you reap a harvest. We learned that a seed is a self-contained unit designed for the reproduction of a species. We discussed the "law of Genesis," which basically explains that everything that God created comes from and reproduces after its own kind. Everything that God created is self-sustaining and self-perpetuating. An apple tree produces apples that contain seeds. These apple seeds produce other trees to come into existence, which produce more apples and more seeds. This represents a self-perpetuating system of apple reproduction. No matter how many apples come from the seeds produced, they all originated from the one. We took a look back to the beginning of creation. God's creation of the heavens and the earth, light, darkness, the sky, oceans, land, grass and every sort of seed-bearing fruit. God also created the moon, stars, sea, and land animals and ultimately man. God planted Adam, the first natural seed, and so we all then come from Adam. Jesus was the first natural and spiritual seed and so to have eternal life we all must be born again in the spirit. God created man in his image and made him master over all. We learned of how God created man and God's plan for the very beginning was for man to live in abundance. It was God's plan that man would lack for nothing. It was God's plan that man's life would be carefree without work or labor. God told man I have given you the seed-bearing plants throughout the earth, and all the fruit trees for your food. God then planted a garden in Eden and placed man in the garden. And God planted all sorts of beautiful trees there in the garden producing the choicest of fruit. At the center of the garden, he placed the tree of life and also the tree of knowledge of good and evil. There was a river that ran through the Garden for the plants and trees. The Lord God placed man in the garden to tend and care for it telling him that he could eat freely from every tree in the garden except from the tree of knowledge of good and evil. He warned Adam that if they ate from that tree then they would surely die. We discussed the fall of man. How Satan entered the Garden of Eden and deceived Eve causing her to eat of the fruit. She also took the fruit to Adam, and he ate of it as well. Because of this disobedience to God and his divine portion, God's plan for man changed. Adam, the first natural seed, ate of the fruit and because he ate of the fruit curses came to us all. These curses included separation from God, death, curses to the soil, and man sweating to make a living from the soil. From there, we moved to discussing the power of a seed and its ability to multiply. Most seeds planted in the soil produce multiple or multiplied new seeds. For example, if you plant a seed of corn in the soil, it will grow a new plant that can have anywhere from one to eight new ears of corn on it. Each of those ears of corn can contain anywhere from two hundred to four hundred new seeds, which is then potentially three thousand and two hundred new seeds! If you were to replant those seeds, you can potentially get ten million two hundred and forty thousand new seeds! This is more than just multiplied but is now exponential growth! This represents the power of a single seed in the Bible! We know that from two people we now have a world population of over seven billion! We also know that the Bible says that just one of us can send one thousand demons to flight but two of us can seed ten thousand demons to flight! That's miraculous multiplication!

In part one of our sermon, we talked about how the scriptures teach us that God knew us before we were in our mother's womb. How he planted us and told us to be fruitful and multiply. This means that we are to bear fruit through the same process that we were created. We bear fruit by sowing. If you don't sow any crops, then you won't produce any harvest. As the word says, we reap what we sow! As an example of this, I showed you in Mark 11 where we looked to the fig tree and saw what happens if we don't produce any fruit. We saw where Jesus was hungry, and he went to the fig tree but found that it had no fruit. Jesus cursed the tree saying that it will never bear fruit again and the tree withered away. I showed you where the gospels say, "For to him who has will more be given and he will have more abundance but from him who has not, been the little he has will be taken away." We are to be fruitful and multiply. We are to produce a harvest. We are to produce fruit and not just any fruit but good fruit! Jesus said that you can tell a tree by its fruit and by the fruit it produces. Every good tree bears good fruit, but a bad tree bears bad fruit.

> **Likewise, every good tree bears good fruit, but a bad tree bears bad fruit. A good tree cannot bear bad fruit, and a bad tree cannot bear good fruit. Every tree that does not bear good fruit is cut down and thrown into the fire. Thus, by their fruit you will recognize them. (Matthew 7:17–20 NIV)**

We learned that there are two types of fruit that we can produce. We can either produce the Fruits of the Spirit or the Fruits of the Flesh. When we follow our sinful nature, the fruit of the flesh, then our lives produce these acts: sexual immorality, impure thoughts, eagerness for lustful pleasure, idolatry and witchcraft; hatred, discord always fighting, jealousy, fits of rage, anger, selfish ambition, always trying to do and get what's best only for you, complaints and criticisms, dissensions, factions, which is groups or clicks and the feeling that everyone else is wrong except those in your own little group. It also says that there will be envy, drunkenness, murder, wild parties, and the like. But when the Holy Spirit controls our lives, or when we allow the Holy Spirit to control our lives, he produces a different fruit in us. The Fruits of the Spirit produce first and foremost love, which is the greatest fruit and gift of all. The other fruits of the spirit are joy, peace, patience, long-suffering, kindness, goodness, faithfulness, gentleness, and self-control.

We learned that fruit doesn't just grow, seeds don't just grow on their own. There is a process to reproduction. Certain things have to happen, certain environments must exist. You have to sow a seed, you have to plant a seed, and that seed needs to have the right elements and conditions to grow. I went over how God created the heavens and the earth with seeds, and he created the environment necessary for the seeds to grow. Seeds won't just grow on their own. They need water and sunlight. They need soil and not just any soil but preferably good soil. As the scriptures and parable we read for the first part of this sermon found in Matthew 13:3–9 showed us, you can sow your seed in many types of soil. Just as there are good and bad seeds, there's good and bad soil.

I told you that Jesus would speak in parables almost as a hidden language so that some wouldn't understand. Some whose hearts were hardened and who were nonbelievers God had cursed them with the curse that they would not hear nor understand. But how blessed are we that our eyes do see, and our ears do hear what thus says the Lord!

And he spake many things unto them in parables, saying, Behold, a sower went forth to sow; And when he sowed, some seeds fell by the way side, and the fowls came and devoured them up: Some fell upon stony places, where they had not much earth: and forthwith they

sprung up, because they had no deepness of earth: And when the sun was up, they were scorched; and because they had no root, they withered away. And some fell among thorns; and the thorns sprung up, and choked them: But other fell into good ground, and brought forth fruit, some an hundredfold, some sixty-fold, some thirtyfold. Who hath ears to hear, let him hear. (Matthew 13:3–9 KJV)

In part 1 of this sermon, we learned from this parable that we needed to have ears that hear so that we will know how to sow our seed in soil to succeed! We learned that we are a seed planted by God to produce, to be fruitful and multiply. The way that we produce is by reproduction through sowing. By planting seeds. We learned the type of fruit that we are to produce, and we know the seeds necessary. We know the seeds that we need to plant. And we learned that we will reap what we sow. If you sow, if you plant hate, then you can expect to reap hatred. If your thoughts aren't pure, then your actions won't be pure, for you will ultimately go where you are thinking! If you're angry or bitter, if you love to fight, if you're selfish, jealous, and can't take criticism. If no one can tell you anything because you're always right and everybody else is wrong outside of you and your click. If all you do is drink, get high, and party like a rock star. If these are the seeds that you sow, then you will produce seeds that do the same! And you will reap all that comes along with what you've sown. Hating men marry hating women that have hating babies and they become all in the hating family!

From the above parable, we then began to look at how the parable switches from the sower and the seed to teaching us about what I want to focus on and continue with in this second part of the series "**Sowing a Seed in Soil to Succeed**," which is the different types of soil upon which the seeds fell. We represent the different types of soil along with the environment or other people that we put ourselves in which affects the fruit that we produce. Since we are the soil that Jesus is speaking of, then it matters what we allow in our ears. It's important that we take time and examine the soil in more detail. There are four different types of soil listed in the parable. The first type of soil mentioned is the wayside. Matthew 13:4 says that some seeds fell by the wayside. Jesus explains the parable by saying that the seed that fell by the wayside represents the heart of a person who hears the Good News about the kingdom and doesn't understand it and so the enemy comes and quickly, easily snatches away the seed from his heart! We talked about how God has a plan for our lives and how Satan wants to destroy that plan just as he did in the Garden of Eden with Adam and Eve. Through this parable, we see the enemy whose plan never changes—steal, kill, destroy. Here we see him in action. In the parable, it says he snatches the seed, the Good News, the Word of God, that the person didn't understand, and so it fell by the wayside where the enemy quickly snatched it up. So what is the wayside? I'm glad you asked! When looking up the definition of wayside, you will find such definitions as:

Wayside

1. The side or edge of a road, way, path, or highway.
2. To *fall by the wayside.* To fail to continue; give up.
3. To *go by the wayside.* To be set aside or discarded because of other considerations, something more important.

I gave you the example of the young man who wanted to follow Jesus. He heard the good news and asked Jesus, "Master, what must I do to be saved?" Jesus told him to go and sell all his possessions, and he walked way. He fell by the wayside. We all know people who tell us all the time how they gon' come to church and get they life right but they just ain't ready. They are still doing whatever it is they do and so they say they ain't gon' come in the church and play with God. They say they ain't gon' come in church and play with God like all the rest of them folks that's in church, them hypocrites is playing. "Naw, I ain't gon' do that!" As if whatever it is that they doing now is more urgent or more important. So the parable says that when the seed fell by the wayside, Satan QUICKLY snatched it up. Even Satan knew its worth. Picture a person dropping some money and quickly picking it up like, "Hey, that's worth something!"

But for the young man that went to Jesus and wouldn't sell his riches, as well as for the person who won't stop whatever it is that they're doing, or whatever it is that's more important, they have fallen by the wayside.

The second type of soil mentioned in the parable is the stony places.

> **Some fell upon stony places, where they had not much earth: and forthwith they sprung up, because they had no deepness of earth: And when the sun was up, they were scorched; and because they had no root, they withered away. (Matthew 13:5–6 KJV)**

Jesus explains the soil referred to as stony places as representing the heart of a man who hears the gospel, the Good News, and receives it with real joy but they turn away because of affliction or persecution. I've sat in many worship services as probably have you, and we've all heard some messages that either moved, grabbed, or convicted you. Have you ever been in service, and it just seemed like the pastor was talking directly to you? I mean they was just all up in your business to the point that you felt like, "Man, somebody had to have tipped him off!" The message just grabbed you and you can't deny that it was a word from God spoken directly to you! But the scriptures say that this person had not much earth. They had no depth, no deepness of earth. He didn't have much depth in his life and so the seed that was sowed though it was received with real joy, the seed didn't root very deeply. We talked in part one about how seeds don't just grow on their own. They need the right environment. They need the right elements and conditions. Roots absorb and transport water, oxygen, and minerals from the soil to the rest of the tree or plant. A tree gets water through its roots. Roots hold a tree in the ground so that the wind can't blow it over. In the Bible, water is symbolic of the Holy Spirit. Psalm 1:3 reads:

And he shall be like a tree planted by the rivers of water, that bringeth forth his fruit in his season; his leaf also shall not wither; and whatsoever he doeth shall prosper. (Psalm 1:3 KJV)

What often happens with new believers to the faith is that being new and coming off the streets where they weren't rooted in the right environment and surrounded by the best elements, they often come tired. They're tired of the life they've been living. They're tired of struggling and doing things their way, and when they finally come to church and hear the Word of God, it gets inside of them, and they accept it with real joy. And even though we wish it could be, we all know that every day is not Sunday morning. Yes, every day is not easy like Sunday morning as Lionel Richie sang. We come to church, but we can't live there. We live out in the real world, and Jesus says that when troubles come or when persecution begins because of your beliefs, the word is new, and the new believer doesn't have much depth. He's coming to church, but he's also going back to his natural environment. Back to his old stomping ground. Back to his old friends and they start asking him where he has been, and he's telling his old friends how he has been going over there to the church house. Now his old friends, you know they ain't got much of any depth to them at all so they ain't really hearing him. They still trying to pass you the bottle or blunt. Come on now, let's keep it real! For a while, you do good, but then living this life and living in this world that we live in we know that troubles will come! I think I'll say that again, troubles will come! When you're not rooted and there's not much depth, you're sprouting up, but you're not deeply rooted and you're not getting enough water. You're only getting water on Sunday mornings, but you're getting dirt thrown on you every day! So when troubles start to come, and the wind starts to blow, or the hot son starts to scorch you, it gets hot! And Jesus says that your enthusiasm fades and you drop out. You wither away.

This is why I believe that one of the most important ministries in the church is new members' ministry. Too often we've seen the enemy attack in this manner. For some people, it took twenty-to-thirty-plus years to get them to Christ and a lot of times people think that once you get to church and make it to the altar and give your life to Christ, some people think that that's going to be the end to all of their problems. Well, I'm sorry but it's not! I wish that Satan gave up that easy, but he doesn't! steal, kill, and destroy! He doesn't give up! He never gives up! So coming to church, giving your life to Christ, and being saved, it doesn't mean that you won't have your share of trials and tribulations. It doesn't mean that you won't go through the winds and storms. God never promised us a life without troubles! Nowhere in the Bible will you find that promise! But he did promise that he would never leave you nor forsake you. He did promise that he would never put more on you than you can bare! He promised you a comforter in the Holy Spirit! He promised you that when the enemy comes in like a flood, that the Holy Spirit of the Lord shall lift up a standard against him! Somebody reading this ought a take ten seconds to thank God for his promises! So we don't grieve, we don't mourn, we don't handle trials and tribulations, problems, like the unsaved do. We don't handle these things like people who have no hope. No, we keep the faith! We keep hope alive! We know that these trials are only to test our faith! David said:

> **Yea, though I walk through the valley of the shadow of death, I will fear no evil: for thou art with me; thy rod and thy staff they comfort me. Thou preparest a table before me in the presence of mine enemies: thou anointest my head with oil; my cup runneth over. Surely goodness and mercy shall follow me all the days of my life: and I will dwell in the house of the LORD for ever. (Psalm 23:4–6 KJV)**

David knew that he was going through the valley! That's a word for somebody reading this! Somebody reading this right now you're going through something. God said to tell you and you need to know that you will not stay there! You will not die there! God said to tell you that you are going through! Say that out loud say, "I'm going through!" I just heard Mrs. Diana Ross, Diana said to tell you that not only are you going through Diana said say, "I'm coming out!"

New member ministry should be one of the most important ministries of the church because when people come to Christ and accept Jesus as their Lord and Savior, once that seed has been planted, the enemy almost always tries to steal that seed before it can become deeply rooted. It's our job to surround our new members and get them involved in orientation classes and to check on them constantly so that we can keep them in a safe environment until that seed has a chance to become deeply rooted.

The third type of soil mentioned in the parable is thorns.

And some fell among thorns; and the thorns sprung up and choked them. (Matthew 13:7 KJV)

In Matthew 13:22, Jesus explains that the ground covered with thistles and thorns represent a man who hears the message but the cares of this life and his longing for money chokes out God's word, and he becomes unfruitful. He does less and less for God. Again, as an example of this, we can look at the young man who wanted to follow God, but he didn't want to part with his riches. Remember, no man can serve two masters! You cannot serve both God and money! For you will love one and hate the other! These are those that care more about the things in this world. The distraction of riches and the natural lust of the world. In the Bible, thorns often represent sin. When Jesus was crucified, we know that they put a crown of thorns on his head. This was fitting as Jesus would bear the sins of the world! The Bible tells us to be in this world but not of this world. Matthew 6:25 says:

Therefore, I tell you, do not worry about your life, what you will eat or drink; or about

your body, what you will wear. Is not life more than food, and the body more than clothes? (Matthew 6:25 NIV)

Satan plants many, many thorns that spring up and choke out the seed of God! Thorns are everywhere! In part 1 of this sermon, I spoke about music and how we need to really listen to what we're listening to instead of just bopping or heads because the beat is catchy. Satan is planting thorns through our music. I love hip-hop! But I must admit that even when I was coming up hip-hop was different. You had just as much or even more positive rap then you had as the mess or garbage hip-hop that we have nowadays. It's some mess out here today! I mean, when I was coming up, you had public enemy, fight the power. You had the X-Clan, this is protected by the red, the black, and the green. You had Heavy D and Rob Base. Before that you had the Sugar Hill Gang. You had the political Tupac. Now don't get me wrong you also had mess like the 2 Live Crew and gangster rap. But back in the day hip-hop was talking about some real stuff. Self-destruction, you're heading for self-destruction! But this mess now, OMG! I ain't even going there! It's all about, sex, money, women, clothes, drugs, guns, and killing each other. It's awful! Thorns!

Lest Satan should get an advantage of us: for we are not ignorant of his devices. (2 Corinthians 2:11 KJV)

Be not ignorant of his devices! Know what your kids are listening to! Know what you are listening to! Know the thorns being planted! I mean even for myself as a full-grown man, I have taken a listen back to some of the songs that I used to sing along with. And now when I hear some of those songs, I can't even sing the lyrics anymore! I know better! Some of this mess is just ignorant! Hip-hop, R & B, pop, rock and roll, all of it! It's thorns choking out the seeds!

I mean, come on, let's keep it real! Some of us go to church and we get a good word, a word that truly broke some yolks and strongholds in our life! Then as soon as we walk out the church and get back in our car the radio or music comes on, "I'm F-R-E-E F N free!" Between you and me, I promise not to tell anybody what you got playing in your car right now. Just that quick, Satan plants thorns. The enemy starts activating his devices to choke out or steal that seed. How about your cell phone? Again, as soon as you walk out the church and check your phone, you got six text messages and two missed calls from…Satan! Lol! Not really Satan, but Satan wants you to instantly get on the phone with your girlfriend or your homeboy that ain't talking about nothing that's gon' water or feed that seed you just received! "Girl, guess who got to fighting last night at the club," or "Girl did you hear about so and so?" Listen, if we are the soil that Jesus is speaking of then we have to protect our environment! We have to be mindful of our conditions! It all matters, and we have to watch what we allow in our ears! This includes television, another of Satan's thorns and devices. Think about all these reality shows showing folks fighting and acting like fools! Fake housewives of wherever! Yeah, I said fake because the only thing that's real about them wives is that they ain't gon' be wives for long! Thorns! Satan is planting thorns everywhere! He's using devices, Facebook, Twitter, Instagram! I'm not saying that everything is from Satan, but Satan will find a way to get into whatever! He will find a way to use and occupy your time! Sometimes you need to get off Facebook and get in HIS BOOK! And what's up with this new generation posting their location and everywhere they at? "We just getting out of church and now we going to Golden Coral." If Satan or any other enemy you might have was looking for you, they wouldn't have no problem finding you! But getting back on track were talking about the soil and sowing a seed in soil to succeed. You have to watch your environment. You have to watch out for the thorns. It's the thorns that choke out the seeds.

The last type of soil that Jesus talks about in the parable is the good soil. This is the type of soil that we should strive to be.

But other fell into good ground, and brought forth fruit, some an hundredfold, some sixtyfold, some thirtyfold. Who hath ears to hear, let him hear. (Matthew 13:8–9 KJV)

The good soil represents those that produce fruit. A seed sown in good soil is multiplied and can produce a bountiful supply of thirty, sixty, and even a hundred times! Remember the "law of Genesis" explains that everything that God created comes from and reproduces after its own kind. Seeds bear fruit, seeds reproduce! God planted you as a seed, and he wants you to produce fruit, good fruit! He wants you to produce fruit of the Spirit!

> **But the fruit of the Spirit is love, joy, peace, longsuffering, gentleness, goodness, faith, Meekness, temperance: against such there is no law. (Galatians 5:22–23 KJV)**

Let's just talk about the greatest of these fruits, love! God wants you to produce love! Now, we all say or claim to love others, but like Mary J Blige, I'm talking about real love! The Bible teaches us what real love is!

> **Love is patient, love is kind. It does not envy, it does not boast, it is not proud. It does not dishonor others, it is not self-seeking, it is not easily angered, it keeps no record of wrongs. Love does not delight in evil but rejoices with the truth. It always protects, always trusts, always hopes, always perseveres. Love never fails. (1 Corinthians 13:4–8a NIV)**

Love, joy, peace, long-suffering, gentleness, goodness, faith, meekness, and temperance. God wants you to sow these seeds! He wants you to sow a good seed just as you were planted as a seed. This is God's purpose for giving us his seed! God is looking for a people to produce spiritual fruit. God said, be fruitful and multiply! Let's put some word to this! In Matthew 7:19, Jesus says that:

> **Every tree that does not bear good fruit is cut down and thrown into the fire. (Matthew 7:19 NIV)**

Psalm 1 says:

> Blessed is the man that walketh not in the counsel of the ungodly, nor standeth in the way of sinners, nor sitteth in the seat of the scornful. But his delight is in the law of the LORD; and in his law doth he meditate day and night. And he shall be like a tree planted by the rivers of water, that bringeth forth his fruit in his season; his leaf also shall not wither; and whatsoever he doeth shall prosper. (Psalm 1:1–3 KJV)

The Vine and the Branches

> "I am the true vine, and my Father is the gardener. He cuts off every branch in me that bears no fruit, while every branch that does bear fruit he prunes so that it will be even more fruitful. You are already clean because of the word I have spoken to you. Remain in me, as I also remain in you. No branch can bear fruit by itself; it must remain in the vine. Neither can you bear fruit unless you remain in me. "I am the vine; you are the branches. If you remain in me and I in you, you will bear much fruit; apart from me you can do nothing. If you do not remain in me, you are like a branch that is thrown away and withers; such branches are picked up, thrown into the fire and burned. If you remain in me and my words remain in you, ask whatever you wish, and it will be done for you. This is to my Father's glory, that you bear much fruit, showing yourselves to be my disciples. "As the Father has loved me, so have I loved you. Now remain in my love. If you

keep my commands, you will remain in my love, just as I have kept my Father's commands and remain in his love. I have told you this so that my joy may be in you and that your joy may be complete. My command is this: Love each other as I have loved you. Greater love has no one than this: to lay down one's life for one's friends. You are my friends if you do what I command. I no longer call you servants, because a servant does not know his master's business. Instead, I have called you friends, for everything that I learned from my Father I have made known to you. You did not choose me, but I chose you and appointed you so that you might go and bear fruit—fruit that will last—and so that whatever you ask in my name the Father will give you. This is my command: Love each other. (John 15 NIV)

Through the parable of Jesus, we can see that seeds play an important role in the spread of the kingdom of God. Seed laws play a key role in understanding the teaching in the parable. In order to sow a seed in soil to succeed, the right seeds need to be sown in the right soil! God's word will always produce more people like God. If you follow God's word, then you will grow and mature to be more like our Lord and Savior who gave us these seed laws. Remember, a seed is a self-contained unit designed for the reproduction of a species. A seed will always produce after its own kind. The planting of God's spiritual seed will always produce a spiritual harvest. God uses people to teach his word as well as show his love. Those that do this are sowing good seeds and glorifying him. The seed of God is not only his word but you! It is the seed of God's word that produces the spiritual fruit in our spirits. When we are born again through the spirit, it comes by accepting and believing God's word as truth. Once we accept this truth, God's seed is rooted in us. The more of the Word of God that you learn, the more seed of God you have inside you, and the more fruit of the Spirit you can produce. It is our job to sow the seeds! It is our job to reproduce, to be fruitful and multiply. You sow so that you can harvest. It is not my word but God's promise that you will reap what you sow! We sow the seed, God makes it grow! God sends the increase! It is not God's will that you lack for anything! Just like with our children, think about how it hurts us to see our kids go without something they need. God's plan for you are as follows:

> **"For I know the plans I have for you,"**
> **declares the** L<small>ORD</small>**, "plans to prosper you and**
> **not to harm you, plans to give you hope and a**
> **future." (Jeremiah 29:11 NIV)**

> **O taste and see that the** L<small>ORD</small> **is good:**
> **blessed is the man that trusteth in him. O fear**
> **the** L<small>ORD</small>**, ye his saints: for there is no want to**
> **them that fear him. The young lions do lack**
> **and suffer hunger: but they that seek the** L<small>ORD</small>
> **shall not want any good thing. (Psalm 34:8–10**
> **KJV)**

God set his plan of abundance for us in the Garden of Eden. God had a system for blessings us. Let's tend to his garden! Let us be good laborer's sowing good seed!

> **The one who plants and the one who**
> **waters have one purpose, and they will each be**
> **rewarded according to their own labor. For we**
> **are co-workers in God's service; you are God's**
> **field, God's building. (1 Corinthians 3:8–9 NIV)**

> **Then saith he unto his disciples, The har-**
> **vest truly is plenteous, but the labourers are**
> **few; Pray ye therefore the Lord of the harvest,**
> **that he will send forth labourers into his har-**
> **vest. (Matthew 9:37–38 KJV)**

Sowing a seed in soil to succeed! May God bless you as a hearer and doer of his word!

Say this prayer:

> *Most Gracious and Heavenly Father, thank you for loving me! Thank you for always caring for me, for always providing for me. Thank you for your plans for my life! Teach me my purpose, Lord. Teach me how to glorify you daily. Teach me how to sow my seed in soil to succeed. To be in position, in right standing in order to be blessed and used by you. Let this word take root in me for your glory. In Jesus's name, amen!*

12

❖

If You Don't Know Me by Now

We have all most likely experienced the unforgettable pain of being hurt by someone really close to us. I am a living witness who can testify that it is not your enemy but rather it is definitely true that the people who are the closest to you have the capability of hurting us the most. I wrote this sermon at a time in my life when I was having a hard time understanding and dealing with the hurt and betrayal from those who I loved the most and would do anything for. I thank God for giving me this word, which freed me from the enemy's attempt and trap of planting a stronghold of unforgiveness in my heart. Enjoy!

> **Jesus answered, "I am the way and the truth and the life. No one comes to the Father except through me. If you really know me, you will know my Father as well. From now on, you do know him and have seen him." Philip said, "Lord, show us the Father and that will be enough for us." Jesus answered: "Don't you know me, Philip, even after I have been among you such a long time?" (John 14:6–9 NIV)**

> **Jesus replied, "Don't you even yet know who I am, Philip, even after all this time I have been with you?" (John 14:9 TLB)**

The title for this sermon is a phrase you might be familiar with, if you don't know me by now. Let me start by sharing a personal testimony, one which you also may have experienced. Have you ever found yourself in a situation of disbelief where you just couldn't believe that someone you love and you've shown and given love, someone you had done and would do anything for, have you ever experienced that person either accusing you or talking to others about you behind your back? Saying such things again, that you just couldn't believe that it was coming out of their mouth! I mean, you couldn't believe that they could fix their mouth to say such things! Especially when it's a lie and you know the truth! When you know that, you have done your best to be a friend to them! Could even be a spouse, mother, father, sister, brother, son, or daughter that you have only tried to love! And not because you wanted something they had or wanted something in return, but simply out of love! I mean, after all, love is an action! Love is not something you can just tell someone. If you truly love someone, you should show it! But to have someone that you love to say something to you or to others that just left you confused like, where did that come from? That's how you feel? That's how you see me? That's how you truly feel about me? If you've even experienced this, then you know how much it hurts! It hurts the same as giving someone your all and having them look at it as if it's nothing or it's not good enough! Even though they still took what you gave but saw it as of no value! They saw it as you doing it for reasons, which you yourself could never even fathom because that's just not you. It's not even in you! And after the hurt, after trying to process how it was that they ever came to their conclusion, finally, it just leaves you at the point where all you can say is, "Hey, if that's how you feel. If that's what you think about me. If you don't know me by now!"

You may remember the title of this sermon. It was a song originally performed by Harold Melvin and the Blue Notes. It was their first hit released as a single in 1972. It was later recorded by Patti Labelle, Simply Red, and others. The first lines of the song are the following:

All the things that we've been through.
You should understand me, like I understand you.

The lyrics really resonated with me because again this is something that I was dealing with. This was something that I was just in disbelief over. This is something that I was praying about and trying to figure out where this had come from. As I was going through the stages of hurt, followed by anger or being upset, you know how we do. "Oh, that's what they on! That's how they want to do me!" "Okay, I'll show 'em!" Well, as I was going through the stages, and as I was thinking about what my response would be, which I have to thank God for doing, because I've grown, and I've learned to never react but respond. Because once upon a time, I would just react! You know what I'm talking about, a lot of us still do, we just react! A reaction is instant, it's off the top! It's anger, it's retaliation! It's blow for blow, eye for eye, or tooth for tooth! A reaction is smack me, and I'll smack you back! This is where Satan thrives by getting us to react to whatever he's showing us! But a response is slow. A response is thought out! A response doesn't just react to what it sees or hears. A response walks by faith and not by sight. A response leads us as the Word of God teaches us to be angry but sin not (Ephesians 4:23).

We see what's going on in the world through the media every day. People are upset! People are angry! That's basically all that the news outlets show us. They show us the protesters but hardly ever the prayers! Satan has a plan! But as I was figuring out how to respond to what I was feeling, and even praying and complaining about it to God. God brought to my remembrance the scriptures! He brought to my attention the writings of John regarding the life of Jesus. Everything that we face, everything that we have ever gone through, everything that we feel, Jesus felt! In fact, he's still feeling it! Our sermon scripture comes from John 14, but if you back up a chapter to John 13, you'll see where it was just before the Passover festival. Jesus knew that the hour had come for him to leave this world and go to be with the Father. You'll see where the devil had already prompted Judas to betray Jesus. In John 13, you will find where Jesus washed his disciples' feet. Jesus was serving them and teaching them to serve! He was teaching them to do as he had done. In John 13:15–17, Jesus says:

**I have set you an example that you should
do as I have done for you. Very truly I tell you,**

**no servant is greater than his master, nor is a
messenger greater than the one who sent him.
Now that you know these things, you will be
blessed if you do them. (John 13:15–17 NIV)**

The same people that Jesus was serving, one of his own disciples,
Jesus knew would betray him! Again, whatever you're dealing with, Jesus
went through it too! He knows! And so, in John 13, Jesus predicted his
betrayal to his disciples. He also predicts another of his disciples, Peter,
denying him, even after Peter told him that he would lay down his life
for him! Just like you've had some folks tell you! "I love you!" "I'll do
anything for you!" "I'll be there whenever you need me!" Jesus predicted
to his disciple Peter that before the rooster crows, you will deny me
three times! And to any of by Bible readers reading this then you know
that's exactly what Peter did! Again, Jesus knows, he's gone through it!

In the passage that we're looking at for this sermon, John 14,
Jesus was still talking to his disciples. At the start of chapter 14, you'll
see where Jesus was comforting his disciples, again knowing what he
was about to endure, and that the hour was near.

Jesus Comforts His Disciples

**"Do not let your hearts be troubled. You
believe in God; believe also in me. My Father's
house has many rooms; if that were not so,
would I have told you that I am going there to
prepare a place for you? And if I go and prepare
a place for you, I will come back and take you to
be with me that you also may be where I am. You
know the way to the place where I am going."**

Jesus the Way to the Father

**Thomas said to him, "Lord, we don't
know where you are going, so how can we
know the way?" Jesus answered, "I am the way**

and the truth and the life. No one comes to the Father except through me. If you really know me, you will know my Father as well. From now on, you do know him and have seen him." Philip said, "Lord, show us the Father and that will be enough for us." Jesus answered: "Don't you know me, Philip, even after I have been among you such a long time?" (John 14 NIV)

I've said it many times in the past; know what you know! Say that out loud to yourself say, "You gotta know!" Yes, you have to know! You can't afford not to know! The stakes are too high! The devil is busy! He's trying to steal your blessings! One mistake can cost you your life! One outburst, one reaction can cost you your livelihood! Everything you've worked so hard for! One bad decision, one sin can cost it all! We've seen it several times both in the media as well as in our own lives. We see it in the Bible, by the sins of one man, Adam, death came to us all! If one sin can curse us for life, then do you know that one act of obedience can set you up for a lifetime! Being able to pass just one test, your next test, can launch you to the next level! Passing this next test can launch you into your destiny! I don't know about you, but I am tired of feeling trapped in my life! I'm tired of feeling like nothing is changing! Like I'm getting nowhere! Does anybody reading this feel the same way? This is what the enemy is telling you! This is what he's showing you! This is why it is important that we know what we know! Know who we know! This is what Jesus was telling his disciples. He was telling them to comfort them. I have to go! I must go! It's good that I go! I'm going to prepare a place for you! And if I go to prepare a place for you, then I will come back and take you to be with me, so that you also may be where I am! (John 14:3). I must go, but I am not leaving you alone! No, in verse 15–17, Jesus promises the Holy Spirit.

Jesus Promises the Holy Spirit

"If you love me, keep my commands. And I will ask the Father, and he will give you

another advocate to help you and be with you forever—the Spirit of truth. (John 14:15–17a NIV)

Does anybody reading this right now know it? You have to know! Know them that labor among you! Jesus knew! He knew who would betray him. He knew who would deny him! And it had to happen! It was a setup! Satan thought he had him! But it was only a setup. Just like the folks that's hating on you! The folks that are talking about you! The folks that mean you no good! The folks that are praying for your downfall! Don't focus too much on that! Don't get too hung up on what others are saying or doing! It's a setup! They are only playing their role! Just like Judas, the one who betrayed Jesus. Just like Peter, the one who denied him. Just like the same ones that crucified Jesus on the cross! But Jesus forgave them! Jesus didn't retaliate, he didn't get even. Jesus said, "Father forgive them, for they know not what they do" (Luke 23:24 KJV). Wow, you have to really get that! You don't always have to retaliate! You don't have to write everybody off! I was sitting here confused and confounded. I was hurt! I was trying to figure out how the ones I love and that are supposed to love me could do this! The ones that are supposed to know me! All the things that we've been through! You should understand me, like I understand you! How could they do this!? But then God revealed to me that, they don't know! They don't always know! They don't know that they are being used! They don't know that Satan is using them. They don't always know that the enemy has crept in! Yes, Satan will creep in! Look, I'll show you!

It was just before the Passover Festival. Jesus knew that the hour had come for him to leave this world and go to the Father. Having loved his own who were in the world, he loved them to the end. The evening meal was in progress, and the devil had already prompted Judas, the son of Simon Iscariot, to betray Jesus. (John 13 NIV)

Jump to Verse 21:

> **After he had said this, Jesus was troubled in spirit and testified, "Very truly I tell you, one of you is going to betray me." His disciples stared at one another, at a loss to know which of them he meant. One of them, the disciple whom Jesus loved, was reclining next to him. Simon Peter motioned to this disciple and said, "Ask him which one he means." Leaning back against Jesus, he asked him, "Lord, who is it?" Jesus answered, "It is the one to whom I will give this piece of bread when I have dipped it in the dish." Then, dipping the piece of bread, he gave it to Judas, the son of Simon Iscariot. As soon as Judas took the bread, Satan entered into him.**

We be so hurt! We be so upset with folks sometimes, knowing how much we love them, and believing that they love us, until whatever fault that happens, happens. And then we are done with them! Forever! We become leery of them, and we build our walls. We no longer trust them. And we often don't forgive them. We spend all of our time fighting with one another, when the word clearly tells us:

> **For we wrestle not against flesh and blood, but against principalities, against powers, against the rulers of the darkness of this world, against spiritual wickedness in high places. (Ephesians 6:12 KJV)**

Judas got a bad rap! We frown on Judas! Judas will always be the traitor! But it was Satan that entered Judas! And it had to happen! Again, it was a setup! Jesus knew that this would happen! In verse 27, Jesus told him, "What you are about to do, do quickly" (John 13:27 NIV). Do it quickly! That's what you ought to tell Satan! That's what you ought to tell your haters, persecutors, criticizers, and condemners! Whatever you are going to do, do it quickly! But look at this, Jesus knew, and yet he still forgave them! Not only did he forgive them, but he also forgave you! Yes, he's forgiven us all, time after time! And in doing so he did it as an example so that we would know that we must forgive one another!

I was hurt! I was upset! Just like what we are seeing all over America right now! Everyone is upset! Many of you reading this are upset! You're upset with loved ones! You're upset with other people! You're upset with yourself! You're upset with what you're going through! You're upset with what you're struggling with! You're upset with where you are in life! Many people are upset with God! They are upset because they don't understand! Because they still don't know! In the passage that we are reading from on today, Jesus was talking to his disciples! He was talking to those who should have known him! They should have known him! Why? Because they had been with him. They had witnessed miracle after miracle, healing after healing. They had sat through teaching after teaching. They witnessed him calm the storm! They witnessed him walk on water! They witnessed Jesus turn water into wine! They witnessed him raise Lazarus from the dead! They witnessed Saul's conversion into Paul! They should have known him! And not only them, not only his disciples, but what about us!? What about all that you have witnessed! What about all that you have seen! What about all that Jesus has brought you through! Time after time! What about the many blessings and miracles he has performed in your life! Just like the disciples, you should know! In John 14, Jesus was both teaching and comforting his disciples. He was telling them:

Let not your heart be troubled: ye believe in God, believe also in me. In my Father's house are many mansions: if it were not so, I would have told you. I go to prepare a place for you. And if I go and prepare a place for you, I will come again, and receive you unto myself; that where I am, there ye may be also. And

whither I go ye know, and the way ye know. (John 14:1–4 KJV)

You should know! Verse 5 changing over to the (NIV):

Thomas said to him, "Lord, we don't know where you are going, so how can we know the way?" Jesus answered, "I am the way and the truth and the life. No one comes to the Father except through me. If you really know me, you will know my Father as well. From now on, you do know him and have seen him."

But look at verse 8, here comes Philip, here comes us! We always want more! Show me more God!

Philip said, "Lord, show us the Father and that will be enough for us." Jesus answered: "Don't you know me, Philip, even after I have been among you such a long time?"

Verse 9 in The Living Bible reads:

Jesus replied, "Don't you even yet know who I am, Philip, even after all this time I have been with you?"

He was asking Philip and today Jesus is asking you! He's telling you, if you don't know me by now!

Picking back up with verse 9 in the NIV:

Anyone who has seen me has seen the Father. How can you say, "Show us the Father"? Don't you believe.

It's all about faith! It's all about what you believe! You have to believe!

Don't you believe that I am in the Father, and that the Father is in me? The words I say to you I do not speak on my own authority. Rather, it is the Father, living in me, who is doing his work. Believe me when I say that I am in the Father and the Father is in me; or at least believe on the evidence of the works themselves.

Is there any evidence? Do we have any evidence reading this right now? Can anybody testify, can anybody say, "I'm evidence, I'm a living witness!" I should have some witnesses reading this! There should be somebody reading this that knows what they know! When you know what you know, no one can tell you otherwise! You've experienced it! You are a living witness! They used to sing in the old church:

It is no secret what God can do
What he's done for others, he'll do for you
With arms wide open, he'll pardon you
It is no secret what God can do!
If you don't know me by now!

When will you know? When will you know Jesus? When will you know Jesus as a redeemer, healer, deliver, as a friend that sticks closer than a brother! As the one who when all others forsake you, when all others fail you, when they turn their back on you, David said,

When my father and my mother forsake me, then the LORD will take me up. (Psalm 27:10 KJV)

When will you know Jesus? As the name above all names! As the one who when can't nobody else help you! When can't nobody else work it out! Jesus will work it out! When will you know? When will you know both who and what you should know! Everyone reading this should know! Blind, crippled, and crazy need to know! The hopeless and the hopeful need to know! No matter your past, background, or where you come from, the Word of God says:

> **That at the name of Jesus every knee should bow, of things in heaven, and things in earth, and things under the earth; And that every tongue should confess that Jesus Christ is Lord, to the glory of God the Father. (Philippians 2:10–11 KJV)**

That's another lesson that we can learn from the disciples. The disciples had different backgrounds, stories, they came from various places and walks of life. Just like us they had different histories including things they used to do and who they used to be. They were fishermen, tax collectors, missionaries, and even killers! What we can learn from that is that it doesn't matter! The Bible teaches us that "whosoever" calls upon the name of the Lord shall be saved! Do you know him? Do you know it? I can't hear you! I don't think we know it! With all that is going on in the world today. With the last days that we might be living in. With all the mess that the media is showing, hatred and division, even from those that are supposed to be our leaders! With folks turning on you left and right, even in your own family! Again, David said, "If it had not been the Lord who was on our side" (Psalm 124:1–2).

David said:

> **I had fainted, unless I had believed to see the goodness of the LORD in the land of the living. Wait on the LORD: be of good courage, and he shall strengthen thine heart: wait, I say, on the LORD. (Psalm 27:13–14 KJV)**

You gotta know! I thank God that I know! That's a blessing! It's a blessing to know!

In the gospels, Jesus said:

> **But blessed are your eyes because they see, and your ears because they hear. For truly I tell you, many prophets and righteous people longed to see what you see but did not see it, and to hear what you hear but did not hear it. (Matthew 13:16–17 NIV)**

It's a blessing because 2 Timothy 3:1–7 says:

> **This know also, that in the last days perilous times shall come. For men shall be lovers of their own selves, covetous, boasters, proud, blasphemers, disobedient to parents, unthankful, unholy, Without natural affection, trucebreakers, false accusers, incontinent, fierce, despisers of those that are good, Traitors, heady, highminded, lovers of pleasures more than lovers of God; Having a form of godliness, but denying the power thereof: from such turn away. For of this sort are they which creep into houses, and lead captive silly women laden with sins, led away with divers lusts, Ever learning, and never able to come to the knowledge of the truth. (2 Timothy 3:1–7 KJV)**

I'm closing, but I thank God for knowing! Not that I know everything or even all that I should, but I thank God that I know what I know! I thank God that I know who I know! That I know that greater is he that is in me than he that is in the world (1 John 4:4) I know that if God be for us, who can be against us (Romans 8:31). I know that he'll never leave me or forsake me! I know Jesus! As long as I know Jesus, that's all I need to know! Just like the disciples, we might not always know which way to go. We might not know which decision to make. We don't always know! We won't always know! We stress ourselves out and drive ourselves crazy trying to figure out how we're going to make it out or make it through! We want to know how! We want God to show us the way! Well, as Jesus told the disciples, "I am the way and the truth and the life. No one comes to the Father except through me" (John 14:6 NIV).

If you don't know me by now!

The door to the kingdom of heaven is open!

If you are not and would like to be saved, it's as easy as one, two, three.

ADMIT that you are a sinner.

For all have sinned and fall short of the Glory of God (Romans 3:23).

BELIEVE in your heart that Jesus Christ is Lord.

For God so loved the world, that he gave his only begotten Son, that whosoever believeth in him shall not perish, but have eternal life (John 3:16).

CONFESS that Jesus is Lord.

For with the heart man believeth unto righteousness, and with the mouth confession is made unto salvation (Romans 10:10).

Say this prayer:

> *Heavenly Father, please forgive me for my sins. I believe that Jesus Christ is my Lord and Savior, your only begotten Son, and that he died for my sins. I ask you to forgive me and to make me a new creation in you. Come into my life, Lord, that I may know you, your purpose, and your way. In Jesus's name, I pray, amen!*

About the Author

Pastor Hasan Smith is a debut author that you will remember from this day forward. He is a gifted writer with a style that captivates readers, leading to knowledge and growth. He is a friend, follower, and servant of God who is passionate about leading others to God. Throughout his life, Hasan has experienced many troubles, trials, and tribulations common to man, which have all lead to him experiencing the faithfulness and love of God, which he wants to share with you. Hasan is married to his lovely wife, Natina, and has two adult children. He was born and raised in Rockford, Illinois, and currently resides in Atlanta, Georgia.

Hasan Smith received his bachelor of science in biblical leadership from Southwestern Christian University where he graduated summa cum laude. He was ordained to preach the gospel of Christ in 2011. He has served in several ministries within the church as well as in multiple areas of leadership including deacon, lead deacon, minister, associate pastor, and pastor. It is throughout his tenure and experiences within the church where he observed how Satan has infiltrated the church creating chaos and confusion using such wiles as religion, traditions, and the concerns of men, which have become a stumbling block to the "true church" and those truly seeking and in need of revelation and a relationship with God.

Printed in the USA
CPSIA information can be obtained
at www.ICGtesting.com
CBHW051831191124
17648CB00035B/392